EDWARD D. ANDREWS

400,000+ SCRIBAL ERRORS
IN THE GREEK NEW
TESTAMENT MANUSCRIPTS

WHAT ASSURANCE DO WE HAVE THAT WE
CAN TRUST THE BIBLE?

400,000+ SCRIBAL ERRORS IN THE GREEK NEW TESTAMENT MANUSCRIPTS

What Assurance Do We Have that We Can Trust the Bible?

Edward D. Andrews

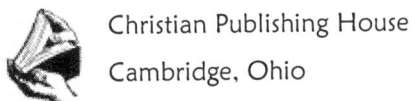

Christian Publishing House

Cambridge, Ohio

Christian Publishing House

Professional Conservative Christian Publishing of the Good News!

CPH Since 2005

Unless otherwise stated, Scripture quotations are from the Updated American Standard Version (UASV) Copyright © 2020 by Christian Publishing House

400,000+ SCRIBAL ERRORS IN THE GREEK NEW TESTAMENT MANUSCRIPTS: What Assurance Do We Have that We Can Trust the Bible? by Edward D. Andrews

ISBN-13: 978-1-949586-92-3

ISBN-10: 1-949586-92-8

From the book Bibliorum Sacrorum Graecus Codex Vaticanus, 1868

4

Table of Contents

INTRODUCTION... 8

The Importance of Being Informed... 9

Discovering the Ehrman Mindset.. 11

Misleading by Failing to Qualify 18

Misleading by Exaggeration 18

Is there a Need for Concern? 19

400,000 to 500,000 Supposed Variants (Errors) in the Manuscripts
.... 20

CHAPTER 1 What Assurances Do We Have that the New Testament
Can Be Trusted.. 23

Critical Study of the Greek New Testament Scriptures................. 23

The Restoration Period 26

The Climax of the Restored Text 27

CHAPTER 2 Why Have Modern Bible Translations Removed Words,
Phrases, Sentences, Even Whole Verses? 29

The Warning from God 29

Copying Manuscripts 30

Some Verses That Should Not Have Ever Been 34

Trusting the Greek New Testament..41

CHAPTER 3 Do We Need the Original Bible Manuscripts?............ 42

How Our Bible Manuscripts Survived the Elements.................... 43

Manuscripts Saved from Egyptian Garbage Heaps..................... 44

CHAPTER 4 How Did Our Bible Manuscripts Survive the Elements?
.... 47

The Materials... 47

Danger from the Elements.. 48

Manuscripts Saved from Egyptian Garbage Heaps.....................51

In the End 52

CHAPTER 5 How Reliable are the Early Texts of the New Testament?
.... 53

Reliable Early Texts of the New Testament 56

CHAPTER 6 Was the New Testament Manuscripts Impacted by the Persecution of Early Christianity? 60

CHAPTER 7 How Did the Spread of Early Christianity Impact the Text of the New Testament 65

The Apostasy 65

Gnostic Beliefs 68

Returning to the First Century 69

CHAPTER 8 The Struggle for a More Accurate Text of the New Testament 81

Wettstein Research Causes Problems 86

CHAPTER 9 Hundreds of Thousands of Mistakes were Made In Copying the Greek New Testament Manuscripts 92

The Greek New Testament Manuscripts 93

CHAPTER 10 How Did the Bible Survive Careless and Even Deceitful Copyists 96

Preservation of Scripture 96

CHAPTER 11 New Testament Textual Criticism and Modern Bible Translation 99

Comparison Results by Score of to What Degree the Reader Is Informed about Textual Issues 110

CHAPTER 12 What Are Textual Variants [Scribal Errors] and How Many Are There? 118

A Simple Example 119

400,000 to 500,000 Supposed Variants in the Manuscripts 120

Miscounting Textual Variants 121

Example of a Textual Variant 124

All Variant Units (Places) 125

Variant Reading and Variation Unit 126

Number of Variants, Significant and Insignificant Variants vs. Level of Certainty 128

Level of Certainty 128

The Entire New Testament (138,020 Words) 131

The Gospels (64,767 Words) 131

The Acts of the Apostles (18,450 Words) 131

The certainty of the Original Words of the Original Authors 135

Related Books by Andrews 139

Bibliography...140

INTRODUCTION

The last 30-50 plus years have seen a rise in interest in what are known as pseudo-gospels, epistles, and apocalypses discovered in the 1950s in Nag Hammadi[1] and other places in Egypt. Generally, these documents and others have been referred to as Gnostic or Apocryphal writings. The term "Gnostic" is a reference to knowledge; especially knowledge of secret spiritual truths, while apocryphally refers to what is hidden or concealed. Both of these terms are used to refer to books that are considered by conservative Christians, as not a part of the inspired authorized canon of Scripture. The writers of these uncanonical works were attempting to emulate the Gospels, Acts, and letters.

The Conspiracy Theory

Because of the liberal scholarship of such persons as Dr. Bart D. Ehrman, Elaine Pagels, Karen L. King, and Marvin W. Meyer; many have become suspicious and skeptical that the Bible is the Word of God and orthodox Christianity, being the Christianity that heresy grew out of centuries later. The Gnostic or Apocryphal writings as presented by the agnostic, atheist, and liberal-to-moderate Bible scholar, to the churchgoers, have created an acceptance never considered by the orthodox community. Both the teachings of Jesus and first-century Christianity have been dealt a new hand in the history books by these writings.

The modern-day scholarship has used these documents to propagate the theory that there was a variety of Christian movements in the first-century, along with what we know as orthodox Christianity, and these varieties just continued to grow until the fourth century. The fourth-century saw the orthodox variety take the prominent position until it was considered the Church. After that, it conspired to erase any evidence that other varieties of Christianity existed in the first-century.

According to these Bible scholars, this conspiratorial church developed the new history that there was only one true Christianity in the first and second century and by the end of the second and beginning of the third-

---

[1] NAG HAMMADI (Någ Hăm ma' dē) Modern Egyptian village 300 miles south of Cairo and about 60 miles north of Luxor or ancient Thebes. Because of the close proximity of Nag Hammadi to the site of an important discovery of ancient documents relating to Gnosticism, the collection of documents is usually referred to as the Nag Hammadi Documents or Library. — Chad Brand, Charles Draper, Archie England et al., Holman Illustrated Bible Dictionary (Nashville, TN: Holman Bible Publishers, 2003), 1167-68.

century division was causing breakaway groups. The new Orthodox Church changed the story around to say that these fragment groups developed in the late second to early third centuries, but never took hold because the orthodox was always the real source of Christianity. This Orthodox Church supposedly suppressed the gnostic and apocryphal writings, while at the same time; they altered what we know to be the canonical Gospels: Matthew, Mark, Luke, and John.

Elaine Pagels, a professor of religion, put it this way,

> Yet even the fifty-two writings discovered at Nag Hammadi offer only a glimpse of the complexity of the early Christian movement. We now begin to see that what we call Christianity, and what we identify as Christian tradition, actually represents only a small selection of specific sources, chosen from among dozens of others. Who made that selection, and for what reasons? Why were these other writings excluded and banned as 'heresy'? What made them so dangerous? Now, for the first time, we have the opportunity to find out about the earliest Christian heresy; for the first time, the heretics can speak for themselves. (Pagels 1989, xxxv)

For scholars like Elaine Pagels and Bart D. Ehrman, Marvin W. Meyer, and others, the Bible is just one source that Christians should look to for their understanding of God. These scholars and others believe that these apocryphal books are just as canonical, authorized and authoritative as the ones we have always accepted, giving further weight to their credibility than the 27 books that have been accepted for almost 2,000 years as the only canonical New Testament. This popular massage is resonating with this generation of Christians that are so busy trying to eke out a living; they do not have the time to investigate the truth of the matter. I believe that our investigation into Bart Ehrman, will add to what other authors have exposed, it is all theory, smoke, and mirrors (deception), nothing more.

The Importance of Being Informed

Almost all Christians today are not as informed about the very book they carry. Sure, many love the Bible, and some see it as the inspired and fully inerrant Word of God. However, let me draw you an analogy. Every Christian also likely believes that the Bible says we are allowed to defend ourselves against physical harm.

Nevertheless, most do not take classes in unarmed self-defense. But then again, some do because they live in rough neighborhoods. Christians that live in high crime areas, where mugging, carjacking, robbery, assault, sexual assault, rape, and murder, are everyday experiences, are more prone to take such classes. Surviving in such a climate may very well depend on their training in unarmed self-defense. It may be the difference between life and death of self, family, friend, or a spiritual brother or sister.

Today we Christians live in a world that assaults the Word of God and Christianity using every possible method. The Bible critic uses such tools as the radio, television, movies, books, schools, billboards, lawsuits, and so on. They are figuratively robbing us, as well as our loved ones with their misleading words, their trickery, their cunning deception, and blatant lies. No place is safe. Do you prepare your Christian children for the onslaught that they face in today's school system? Do you prepare yourself? One may believe that they do not need to defend what they know to be true, but that does not always end with the best results, as many are walking away from the faith, as we saw from the above.

Suppose you are online on a Christian discussion group on Facebook or Twitter, and someone begins raising doubts about the Bible. The issues they raise cannot just be set aside because Christians new in their faith may be on the group with you. If none of the Christians on the discussion group defends the Bible against the critic, the new Christians may assume we have no answers and start reading books, which lead them into a spiritual shipwreck. This too is a matter of life and death, eternal life. Moreover, listen to Peter's words, as he spells out our obligation as Christians, "in your hearts honor Christ the Lord as holy, **always being prepared to make a defense** to anyone who asks you for a reason for the hope that is in you."– 1 Peter 3:15.

William Lane Craig writes, "I think the church is really failing these kids. Rather than provide them training in the defense of Christianity's truth, we focus on emotional worship experiences, felt needs, and entertainment. It's no wonder they become sitting ducks for that teacher or professor who rationally takes aim at their faith. In high school and college, students are intellectually assaulted with every manner of non-Christian philosophy conjoined with an overwhelming relativism and skepticism. We've got to train our kids for war. How dare we send them unarmed into an intellectual war zone? Parents must do more than take their children to church and read them Bible stories. Moms and dads need to be trained in apologetics themselves and so be able to explain to their children simply from an early age and then with increasing depth why we believe as we do. Honestly, I find it hard to understand how Christian couples in our day and age can risk bringing children into the world without being trained in apologetics as part of the art of parenting."[2]

---

[2] Craig, William Lane. On Guard: Defending Your Faith with Reason and Precision (Kindle Locations 267-274). David C. Cook. Kindle Edition.

Craig also writes, "If the gospel is to be heard as an intellectually viable option for thinking men and women today, then it's vital that we as Christians try to shape American culture in such a way that Christian belief cannot be dismissed as mere superstition. This is where Christian apologetics comes in. If Christians could be trained to provide solid evidence for what they believe and good answers to unbelievers' questions and objections, then the perception of Christians would slowly change. Christians would be seen as thoughtful people to be taken seriously rather than as emotional fanatics or buffoons. The gospel would be a real alternative for people to embrace. I'm not saying that people will become Christians because of the arguments and evidence. Rather I'm saying that the arguments and evidence will help to create a culture in which Christian belief is a reasonable thing. They create an environment in which people will be open to the gospel. So becoming trained in apologetics is one way, a vital way, of being salt and light in American culture today."

A Look Into Ehrman's Claim of 400,000+ Textual Errors

This publication will be dealing with the Greek text of our New Testament, through the Eyes of Dr. Bart D. Ehrman, in his New York Times bestseller: *Misquoting Jesus: The Story Behind Who Changed the Bible and Why* (2005). First, in this preface, we will look into Bart D. Ehrman's early life and spiritual decline as he moved from being an Evangelical conservative Christian to becoming an agnostic. Second, we will open with some introductory chapters on the basics of New Testament textual studies and the trustworthiness, as well as some insights that will help us better understand Bible difficulties. Third, we will give the reader the fundamentals of some of Ehrman's arguments. Fourth, we will offer some thoughts on how to view these claims.

Before beginning, we are going to approach this book, by assuming that every reader has no knowledge of the subject matter of Bible difficulties and textual studies. In other words, we will be defining and explaining many things. The reason for this approach is, Ehrman's book is written on a popular level, meaning that his audience is churchgoers and laypersons, who in all likelihood have never read a book on textual criticism or Bible difficulties. This does not mean we will neglect the deeper things because these will also be addressed, on a layperson level as well.

Discovering the Ehrman Mindset

My questions were complicated even more as I began to think increasingly about the manuscripts that conveyed the words. The more I studied Greek, the more I became interested in the manuscripts that preserve the New Testament for us, and in the science of textual criticism, which can **supposedly** help us reconstruct what the <u>original</u> words of the New Testament were. I kept reverting to my basic question: how does it help us to say that the Bible is the inerrant word of God if in fact we don't have the words copied by the scribes—sometimes correctly but sometimes **(many times!)** incorrectly? What good is it to say that the autographs (i.e., the <u>originals</u>) were inspired? *We* don't have the <u>original</u>! We have **only error ridden copies**, and the **vast majority of these are centuries removed from the <u>originals</u> and different from them, evidently, in thousands of ways.** Bold mine. (Ehrman, 2005, p. 7)

Please notice the mental disposition, "supposedly," "many times!" "don't have the originals!" "error ridden copies," the "vast majority of," "centuries removed," "different from," and "thousands of." Well, this certainly sounds quite ominous, does it not? We might all throw up our hands and go home, and give up Christianity because we could never possess the Word of God in the New Testament. Do not my latter words sound a bit sarcastic toward Ehrman? Yes, they are meant to come across that way, because I had the agenda to be sarcastic. The point being, one can tell the intent of what is being expressed by the wording. Now, what would we think Ehrman's objective is, by the way, he is writing in the above? We will get back to that soon enough.

The above quote comes from Bart D Ehrman's bestseller *Misquoting Jesus: the Story behind Who Changed the Bible and Why*. Bart D. Ehrman is actually a New Testament scholar extraordinaire. He chairs the department of religious studies at the University of North Carolina, Chapel Hill. He is one of the world's leading authorities on early Christianity and the life of Jesus Christ. He has authored over twenty books in this field of study.

Moreover, his books are New York Times bestsellers. Ehrman was raised in a conservative Christian family of five in the heartland of America—Lawrence, Kansas. It was the 1950s and 1960s, a time when the American citizens took religion very seriously.

His early life was filled with a conservative Christian influence. Christian youth camp and a camp leader that he calls "Bruce" influenced his middle teens. It was here that Ehrman was moved by his 'born-again' experience to take the Bible more serious. Therefore, the next stage was all too natural, he signed on at Moody Bible Institute in 1973, a conservative religious institution that takes Bible education serious in the extreme. The school name itself carries a reputation of knowing that it educates nothing but the most skilled Christians, who accept the Bible as nothing short of fully inerrant, with every word being inspired of God. In his telling of his early life, Ehrman reveals that he was not such a student, as he was very worried as he got to know that there were no autograph manuscripts still extant (available today).[3]

Even more disturbing to him was that textual scholars do not even have the first published copies of the autographs or the second and third generation of copies. This issue alone seemed to push Ehrman into the field of textual studies. This weighed heavy on his young mind as he entered yet another evangelical university of extraordinary reputation in producing some of the best scholars the world has to offer: Wheaton College. Wheaton, being conservative, seemed though to pale in comparison to his former days at Moody. It was now time to peak outside of the box of just accepting things and not raising any issues about discrepancies that had been plaguing his mind. It was here that he met scholars, who were not afraid of asking the tough questions concerning their faith. While this is certainly reasonable, it was one more step toward the slippery slope that was going to consume young Ehrman. It was here that we see the mindset of Ehrman starting to develop, as our initial quote at the outset of this piece, in the above.

As he settled into the field of textual criticism, Ehrman would head on to yet another big named school, but one that was now moving away from his founding conservative principles, to a more liberal progressive stance: Princeton Theological Seminary. It is here that Bart D. Ehrman would study under the renowned textual scholar, Bruce M. Metzger. When writing an initial paper, for a Princeton professor by the name of Cullen Story at the beginning of his stay, Bart tried to give a long, complicated answer to overturn a discrepancy found in the Gospel of Mark. (Mark 2:26; 1 Sam 21:1-6) It was the response of this professor, on Bart's paper, which sent Ehrman onto the road of Agnosticism: "Maybe Mark just made a mistake." Here is Bart's established mindset from *Misquoting Jesus* before he even enters his first chapter,

> **Page 7**: How does it help us to say that the Bible is the inerrant word of God if in fact we don't have the words of God inerrantly inspired, but only the words copied by the scribes - sometimes correctly, but sometimes (many times!) incorrectly?

---

[3] The manuscript penned by one of the New Testament writers: Matthew, Mark, Luke John, Paul, Peter, James, or Jude. However, it may not have been personally penned, as the writer may have dictated to a scribe, as he took things down in shorthand, to later create a rough draft, which would be corrected by the Bible writer ad scribe, before being signed and published.

Page 10: It is one thing to say that the originals were inspired, but the reality is that we don't have the originals - so saying they were inspired doesn't help me much.

Page 10: Not only do we not have the originals, we don't have the originals of the first copies. We don't even have copies of the copies of the originals, or copies of the copies of the copies of the originals.[4]

Page 11: If one wants to insist that God inspired the very words of scripture, what would be the point if we don't have the very words of scripture? In some places, as we will see, we simply cannot be sure that we have constructed the original text accurately. It's a bit hard to know what the words of the Bible mean if we don't even know what the words are!

Page 11: The fact that we don't have the words surely must show, I reasoned, that he did not preserve them for us. And if he didn't perform that miracle, there seemed to be no reason to think that he performed the earlier miracle of inspiring those words.

It seems that Ehrman has a mindset that is perpetuated by a blind spot, the fact that we do not have the originals. Here in the introduction, we will start with Ehrman's obstacle of Mark 2:26, as this was the catalyst that sent him over the edge. At Mark 2:26, many translations have Jesus saying that David went into the house of God and ate the showbread "when Abiathar was high priest." Since Abiathar's father, Ahimelech was the high priest when that event took place; such a translation would seem to result in a historical error.

As Ehrman explains his assignment of having to write a paper dealing with the discrepancy of Mark 2:26: 'he was overly concerned with the idea of turning in anything that did not keep the validity of inerrancy alive.' He said he had to do "fancy exegetical foot-work" for that to happen. The context of his recounting of the story was that he had to bend heaven and earth to get something resembling an explanation that avoided a historical error, which was not only a daunting task but time-consuming as well. Ehrman writes,

At the end of my paper, [Professor Story] wrote a simple one-line comment that for some reason went straight through me. He wrote: "Maybe Mark just made a mistake." I started thinking about it, considering all the work I had put into the paper, realizing that I had to do some pretty fancy exegetical

---

[4] This may very well be an exaggeration because we do have some very early papyri.

foot-work to get around the problem, and that my solution was in fact a bit of a stretch. I finally concluded, "Hmm . . . maybe Mark *did* make a mistake."

Once I made the admission, the floodgates opened. For if there could be one little, picayune mistake in Mark 2, maybe there could be mistakes in other places as well.... This kind of realization coincided with the problems I was encountering the more closely I studied the surviving Greek manuscripts of the New Testament. It is one thing to say that the original were inspired, but the reality is that we do not have the originals—so saying they were inspired doesn't help much, **unless I can reconstruct the originals.**[5]

Before looking at Ehrman's "fancy exegetical footwork" that he says, 'took much work,' let us say that this Bible difficulty is solved with simple reasoning. Is it not true that if we referred to the Roman Emperor Tiberius, before the time of his becoming emperor, we would say Roman Emperor Tiberius? Why? Because it is a title and position that he is known for throughout history. This would hold true with Abiathar as well. Therefore, Mark's reference to Abiathar as high priest is simply a reference to the position he had in history.

Mark 2:26 (NET): "he [being David] entered the house of God when Abiathar was high priest." This rendering is certainly a historical error if taken outside of the way we normally talk about people in history. Let us start with looking at an interlinear, to get an understanding of the Greek words involved.

ΚΑΤΑ ΜΑΡΚΟΝ 2:26 1881 Westcott-Hort New Testament (WHNU)[6]

How he went into into the house of the God on Abiathar
26 πῶς   εἰσῆλθεν   εἰς τὸν οἶκον   τοῦ   θεοῦ ἐπὶ ʼΑβιάθαρ
chief priest and the loaves of the presentation he ate which not
ἀρχιερέως καὶ τοὺς ἄρτους τῆς   προθέσεως ,ἔφαγεν, οὓς οὐκ

---

[5] Ehrman, Bart D.: Misquoting Jesus: The Story Behind Who Changed the Bible and Why. New York: HarperCollins, 2005, pp. 9-10.

[6] WHNU stands for the master critical Westcott and Hort Greek text of 1881, the 27th edition of the Nestle-Aland Greek text of 1993 and the fourth edition of the United Bible Societies Greek text of 1993. Of course, WH alone would refer to Westcott and Hort, while NA27 alone would stand for the Nestle-Aland text and UBS4 alone would stand for the United Bible Societies Greek text.

it is lawful to eat if not the priests and he gave also to the ones
ἔξεστιν   φαγεῖν εἰ μὴ τοὺς ,ἱερεῖς, καὶ ἔδωκεν καὶ   τοῖς

together with him being?
σὺν   αὐτῷ οὖσιν;

The Greek structure of Mark 2:26 is similar to that of Mark 12:26 and has been used by the translations below in their rendering of 2:26. This is perfectly acceptable, and there was no need for any "fancy exegetical footwork." The only exegetical footwork that I see is Ehrman's attempt at exaggerating a small Bible difficulty and not giving the complete picture. One has to keep in mind that original readers did not need to go to the length that we do today. It was written to them, in their language and their historic setting. We are 2,000 years removed and in a modern era that can hardly relate to them. Therefore, in translation and exegesis, there is work to be done. Yet, any beginning Bible student with the reference works could have resolved this Bible difficulty in a matter of minutes. In fact, any churchgoer with the *Big Book of Bible Difficulties* by Norman Geisler or the *Encyclopedia of Bible Difficulties* by Gleason L. Archer could have found a reasonable answer the moment they opened the book. Why Ehrman struggled so when he had three years at Moody Bible Institute and two years at Wheaton College is beyond this writer.

Mark 12:26 (USB4):

  on the thornbush how
26 ... ἐπὶ τοῦ   βάτου   πῶς ...

Mark 12:26: epi tou batou ["*in the time of* the burning bush"]

Mark 2:26 (NASB): "in the time of Abiathar"

Mark 2:26 (ESV): "in the time of Abiathar"

Mark 2:26 (HCSB): "in the time of Abiathar"

Mark 2:26: (ἐπὶ Ἀβιαθὰρ) epi abiathar ["*in the time of* Abiathar"]

Mark 12:26: (ἐπὶ τοῦ βάτου) epi tou batou ["*in the time of* the burning bush"]

Luke 20:37: (ἐπὶ τῆς βάτου) epi tes batou ["*in the time of* the burning bush"]

Acts 11:28: (ἐπὶ Κλαυδίου) epi klaudiou ["*in the time of* Claudius"]

Hebrews 1:2: (ἐποίησεν τοὺς αἰῶνας) epoiesen tous aionas ["*in the time of* the last days."]

Actually, if we look at Jesus' words: "He [David] entered the house of God, in the time of Abiathar the high priest, and ate the bread of the Presence;" Jesus did not state that Abiathar was high priest at the time of this incident, only "in the time of . . ."[7] Contextually, Abiathar is actually present when the event took place. And in the story just after the murder of his father and would be high priest, a position, and title of which one would refer to him as thereafter, even in discussing events before his receiving that position. This is just a loose citation of Scripture. Today, we do it all the time. Therefore, it was in the time of Abiathar, but not during the time, he occupied the chief priest position. – 1 Sam 22:9-12, 18; 23:6; 1 Sam 21:1-6; 22:18-19.

This is actually the argument that Ehrman had given to his professor, Cullen Story, which is a reasonable argument. Here are Ehrman's own words,

> In my paper for Professor Story, I developed a **long and complicated** argument to the effect that even though Mark indicates this happened "when Abiathar was the high priest," it doesn't really mean that Abiathar was the high priest, **but that the event took place in the part of the scriptural text** that has Abiathar as one of the main characters. My argument was based on the meaning of the Greek words involved and was a bit convoluted. *Misquoting Jesus* (p. 9)

Ehrman believes that his argument to Professor Story was "long and complicated argument." Ehrman says that his argument was also "convoluted," which means that it was extremely intricate: too complex or intricate to understand easily. The above argument is made in one page of typed text and wrote on a level that could be easily understood. I do not personally see it as "long and complicated," nor "convoluted." Sadly, it gets even worse for Ehrman and his case, because he actually expresses himself in the same way that Jesus did, which is a common way of expressing things. If we look at page 9, the very page of his complaint, we will find Ehrman saying:

> Jesus wants to show the Pharisees that "Sabbath was made for humans, not humans for the Sabbath" and so reminds them of what the great **King David** had done when he and his men were hungry, how they went into **the Temple** "when Abiathar was the high priest" and ate the show bread, which was only for the priests to eat. *Misquoting Jesus* (p. 9)

---

[7] Ἀβιαθὰρ ἀρχιερέως *under, in the time of, Abiathar the high priest* **Mk 2:26.** ἐ. ἀρχιερέως Ἄννα καὶ Καιάφα **Lk 3:2.** ἐ. Κλαυδίου **Ac 11:28**

First, David was **not the king at the time** of Ehrman's reference. Second, there was **no Temple at the time** it was the Tabernacle. This is just a loose reference to Scripture by Ehrman as he refers to the person and place involved. We know David as King David, so we are not befuddled by his loose reference and recognize this is a way of referencing things. He also knows we think of it as a Temple, not the Tabernacle; we generally think of the Tabernacle being associated with Moses. Moreover, it was David's son, Solomon, who would eventually build the Temple. Here we have a world-renowned Bible scholar, who uses a loose reference in his book, and expects that his audience will understand what he means by his way of wording things. Was Ehrman technically chronologically wrong? Yes, in the strictest sense of things, if one wishes to be unreasonable. However, if we recognize this is an acceptable way of human expression; then, no really, he is not wrong because he knows his audience will understand his loose reference, and so it goes with Jesus as well. If only, Ehrman was as reasonable with Mark, who was recording Jesus' words.

Misleading by Failing to Qualify

If a textual scholar writes a book and says that the NT Greek manuscripts contain 400,000+ errors or variants without qualifying that statement, this alone can be quite staggering to think about and will undoubtedly dishearten the reader. A fuller explanation of how we count variants will be given in a later chapter 'What Are Textual Variants (Errors) and How Many Are There?'

The critical text is as close as we get to what the original would have been like (99.95% restored).[8] Therefore, we use the reading in the critical text as the original reading, and anything outside of that in the manuscript history is a variant: 'spelling, word order, omission, addition, substitution, or a total rewrite of the text.'

Misleading by Exaggeration

For example sake alone: if we find numerous overdone statements and exaggerated explanations, with missing information and many exclamation points to emphasize the negative, but seldom mentioning the positive; we can eventually see **a pattern.** If this proves to be the case, the writer is certainly doing a disservice to the reader. If we find 200 texts that

---

[8] While it is true that some scholars, like Philip Comfort, argue that, the NU could be improved upon, because in many cases it is too dependent on internal evidence when the documentary evidence should be more of a consideration as to the weightiness of the matter. Again though, this is a handful of places, when one considers 138,020 words in the Greek New Testament.

are supposed to be full of historical, geographical, or scientific errors, and they are highlighted, yet this person fails to explain to the reader that each of the 200 errors have reasonable and logical explanations; then, this is a pattern of misleading the reader by failing to disclose all of the facts. Many who have read Ehrman's *Misquoting Jesus* are simply churchgoers that occasionally study the Bibles, who are not aware of the apologetic answers to the claims. Scholars are hardly moved by them, as they are well aware of the alternative explanations.

If we find repeated behavior that reflects an agenda of highlighting minute issues, while ignoring a massive amount of positives, one can hardly avoid the conclusion that we have an agnostic scholar, who wishes others to join his ranks. Why dramatically point to Mark 2:26 as the obstacle with the exclamation points and act as though the historical error is a fact, and only "fancy exegetical footwork" can possibly undo it? Each of Ehrman's textual issues has explanations that he mostly fails to share with his reader. Let us look at one more text before moving on.

Mark 4:31 Updated American Standard Version (UASV)

[31] It is like a grain of mustard seed, which, when sown on the ground, is the smallest of all the seeds on earth,

Critic: Today, we know that the mustard seed is not the smallest seed on earth. If Jesus were the Son of God, he would have known that.

Bart D. Ehrman: "Jesus says later in Mark 4 that the mustard seed is 'the smallest of all seeds on the earth,' maybe I don't need to come up with a fancy explanation for how the mustard seed is the smallest of all seeds when I know full well it isn't"—p. 9-10.

Some commentators argue that Jesus was referring to the seed for the black mustard plant. However, while this could be the case, it need not be that complicated. Jesus was talking to Jewish farmers, to which the mustard seed was the smallest. Jesus was not giving a lesson in botany but was attempting to make a point by using what the people knew. In fact, the mustard seed is one of the tiniest seeds, and to those, to whom Jesus was speaking to, it was. The Bible is not a science textbook, nor is to be treated as such in our interpretation.

Is there a Need for Concern?

Is there a pattern forming here? Is the problem anything more than a Bible difficulty for the regular churchgoer, who has the potential to find a reasonable answer within minutes? Does Ehrman's expression "fancy explanation" imply more than one needing some Bible background knowledge that takes less than five minutes to acquire? To this writer, it does, when considered with his other phrase that we have already seen. Ehrman said that he had to do "some pretty fancy exegetical footwork to get around the problem, [of Mark 2:26's 'when Abiathar was high priest'] and in fact, my solution was a bit of a stretch." Our above answer is accepted by some of the best translations and commentators, as well as apologists was found within a few minutes.[9] There was no deed for some "fancy exegetical footwork." It seems that Bart D Ehrman, the "happy agnostic" as he calls himself is attempting to make his points in exaggerated fashion in *Misquoting Jesus*. A person that intends to exaggerate his claims allow '**some** manuscripts' to become '**the majority** of manuscripts,' and **the 'majority** of manuscripts' becoming '**all manuscripts**,' and '**some cases** of intentional errors by scribes' becomes '**all cases**.' One certainly has to question the credibility of any scholar who would tend to exaggerate numbers, extent, reports, and leave out other information that would derail his point. We need to keep the phrase "**accuracy of statement**" in mind.

400,000 to 500,000 Supposed Variants (Errors) in the Manuscripts

With this abundance of evidence, what can we say about the total number of variants known today? Scholars differ significantly in their estimates—some say there are 200,000 variants known, some say 300,000, some say **400,000 or more!** We do not know for sure because, despite impressive developments in computer technology, no one has yet been able to count them all. Perhaps, as I indicated earlier, it is best simply to leave the matter in comparative terms. There are more variations among our manuscripts than there are words in the New Testament.[10]

Bart D. Ehrman has some favorite, unprofessional ways of describing the problems, which he stresses without qualification, in every interview he has for a lay audience or seminary students. Below are several, the first two from the quotation above:

---

[9] Gleason L. Archer Jr.: *Encyclopedia of Bible Difficulties*. Grand Rapids, MI: Zondervan, 1984, p. 329;
[9] Norman L. Geisler; Thomas Howe: *The Big Book of Bible Difficulties*. Grand Rapids, MI: Baker Books, 1992, p. 345; Kaiser, Walter C.; Davids, Peter H.; Bruce F. F.; Brauch, Manfred T.: Hard Sayings of the Bible. Downer Groves, Illinois: InterVarsity Press, 1996, pp 411-412; Comfort, Philip W.: New Testament Text and Translation Commentary. Carol Stream, Illinois: Tyndale House Publishers, 2008, p. 102

[10] Ibid., 89-90

- Scholars differ significantly in their estimates—some say there are 200,000 variants known, some say 300,000, some say **400,000 or more!**

- There are **more variations** among our manuscripts **than there are words** in the New Testament.

- We have only **error-ridden copies**, and the vast majority of these are centuries removed from the originals and different from them, evidently, in thousands of ways. (*Whose Word is It*, 7)

- We don't even have copies of the copies of the originals, or **copies of the copies of the copies of the originals.** (*Misquoting Jesus*, 10)

- **In the early Christian centuries, scribes were amateurs** and as such were more inclined to alter the texts they copied. (*Misquoting Jesus*, 98)

- **We could go on nearly forever** talking about specific places in which the texts of the New Testament came to be changed, either accidentally or intentionally. (*Misquoting Jesus*, 98)

- The Bible began to appear to me as a very **human book.** (*Misquoting Jesus*, 11)

Each of the bullet points above claimed by Ehrman can be categorized as an exaggeration, misinformation, misleading, or just a failure to be truthful. Many laypersons-churchgoers have been spiritually shipwrecked in their faith by such unexplained hype. What the uninformed person hears is that we can never get back to the originals or even close, that there are hundreds of thousands of significant variants that have so scarred the text, we no longer have the Word of God, and it is merely the word of man. How such a knowledgeable man cannot know the impact his words are having is beyond this author.

Daniel B. Wallace is the Executive Director of CSNTM & Senior Research Professor of NT Studies at Dallas Theological Seminary. Wallace is a conservative evangelical scholar who offers us some insights on Ehrman's claims.

The approximately 400,000 textual variants among New Testament manuscripts, many who read *Misquoting Jesus* get the impression that this one datum is enough to destroy the Christian faith. But the reality is that less than one percent of all variants are both meaningful and viable. And even Ehrman himself has admitted that no cardinal doctrine is jeopardized by these variants.[11]

Before we offer an extensive easy to understand apologetic answer to the issue of how we can have 400,000+ textual errors in the Greek New Testament that only has about 138,600 words and at the same time say that we can trust it as the Word of God, we will offer the reader several introductory chapters.

---

[11] Retrieved Monday, August 19, 2019

CHAPTER 1 What Assurances Do We Have that the New Testament Can Be Trusted

In the Christian Greek New Testament Scriptures, many copyists have exercised great care in copying their manuscripts. However, we would be remiss if we did not say that some copyists were inexperienced or took certain liberties with the text that they were copying, so we have ended up with a number of scribal errors in the Greek New Testament manuscripts. Mostly, these scribal errors are insignificant and have no bearing on the integrity of the Bible. These scribal errors have been detected and corrected by the careful and meticulous work of hundreds of textual scholars as they have compared tens of thousands of original language manuscripts and ancient versions.

Critical Study of the Greek New Testament Scriptures

The Dark Ages (5th to 15th centuries C.E.),[12] was a time when the Church had the Bible locked up in the Latin language, and scholarship and learning were nearly nonexistent. However, with the birth of the Morning Star of the Reformation, John Wycliffe (1328-1384), and the invention of the printing press in 1455, the restraints were loosened, and there was a

---

[12] B.C.E. means "before the Common Era," which is more accurate than B.C. ("before Christ"). C.E. denotes "Common Era," often called A.D., for anno Domini, meaning "in the year of our Lord."

rebirth of interest in the Greek language. Moreover, with the fall of Constantinople to the Turks in 1453 C. E., many Greek scholars and their manuscripts were scattered abroad, resulting in a revival of Greek in the Western citadels of learning.

About fifty years later, or at the beginning of the sixteenth century, Ximenes, archbishop of Toledo, Spain, a man of rare capability and honor, invited foremost scholars of his land to his university at Alcala to produce a multiple-language Bible—not for the common people, but for the educated. The outcome would be the Polyglot, named Complutensian, corresponding to the Latin of Alcala. This would be a Bible of six large volumes, beautifully bound, containing the Old Testament in four languages (Hebrew, Aramaic, Greek, and Latin) and the New Testament in two (Greek and Latin). For the Greek New Testament, these scholars had only a few manuscripts available to them, and those of late origin. One may wonder why this was the case when they were supposed to have access to the Vatican library. This Bible was completed in 1514, providing the first printed Greek New Testament, but it did not receive approval by the pope to be published until 1520 and was not released to the public until 1522.

Froben, a printer in Basel, Switzerland became aware of the completion of the Complutensian Polyglot Bible and of its pending consent by the pope to be published. Immediately, he saw a prospect of making profits. He at once sent word to Erasmus, who was the foremost European scholar of the day and whose works he had published in Latin, pleading with him to hurry through a Greek New Testament text. In an attempt to bring the first published Greek text to completion, Erasmus was only able to locate, in July of 1515, a few late cursive manuscripts for collating and preparing his text. It would go to press in October of 1515 and would be completed by March of 1516. In fact, Erasmus was in such a hurried mode that he rushed the manuscript containing the Gospels to the printer without first editing it, making such changes as he felt were necessary on the proof sheets. Because of this terrible rush job, the work contained hundreds of typographical errors, as we noted earlier. Erasmus himself admitted this in his preface, remarking that it was "rushed through rather than edited." Bruce Metzger referred to the Erasmian text as a "debased form of the Greek Testament." (B. M. Metzger 1964, 1968, 1992, 103)

As one would expect, Erasmus was moved to produce an improved text in four succeeding editions of 1519, 1522, 1527, and 1535. Erasmus' editions of the Greek text, we are informed, ultimately proved an excellent achievement, even a literary sensation. They were inexpensive, and the first two editions totaled 3,300 copies, in comparison to the 600 copies of the large and expensive six-volume Polyglot Bible. In the preface to his first edition, Erasmus stated, "I vehemently dissent from those who would not have private persons read the Holy Scriptures, nor have them translated into the vulgar tongues." (Baer 2007, 268)

Except for everyday practical consideration, the editions of Erasmus had little to vouch for them, for he had access only to five (some say eight) Greek manuscripts of relatively late origin, and none of these contained the entire Greek New Testament. Rather, these comprised one or more sections into which the Greek texts were normally divided: (1) the Gospels; (2) Acts and the general epistles (James through Jude); (3) the letters of Paul; and (4) Revelation. In fact, of the some 5,750 Greek New Testament manuscripts that we now have, only about fifty are complete.

Consequently, Erasmus had but one copy of Revelation (twelfth-century). Since it was incomplete, he merely retranslated the missing last six verses of the book from the Latin Vulgate back into Greek. He even frequently brought his Greek text in line with the Latin Vulgate; this is why there are some twenty readings in his Greek text not found in any other Greek manuscript.

Martin Luther would use Erasmus' 1519 edition for his German translation, and William Tyndale would use the 1522 edition for his English translation. Erasmus' editions were also the foundation for later Greek editions of the New Testament by others. Among them were the four published by Robert Estienne (Stephanus, 1503-59). The third of these, published by Stephanus in 1550, became the Textus Receptus or Received Text of Britain and the basis for the King James Version. This took place through Theodore de Beza (1519-1605), whose work was based on the corrupted third and fourth editions of the Erasmian text. Beza would produce nine editions of the Greek text, four being independent (1565, 1589, 1588-9, 1598), and the other five smaller reprints. It would be two of Beza's editions, that of 1589 and 1598, which would become the English Received Text.

Beza's Greek edition of the New Testament did not even differ as much as might be expected from those of Erasmus. Why do I say, as might be expected? Beza was a friend of the Protestant reformer, John Calvin, succeeding him at Geneva, and was also a well-known classical and biblical scholar. In addition, Beza possessed two important Greek manuscripts of the fourth and fifth century, the D and D^p (also known as D^2), the former of which contains most of the Gospels and Acts as well as a fragment of 3 John, and the latter containing the Pauline epistles. The Dutch Elzevir editions followed next, which were virtually identical to those of the Erasmian-influenced Beza text. It was in the second of seven of these, published in 1633 that there appeared the statement in the preface (in Latin): "You therefore now have the text accepted by everybody, in which we give nothing changed or corrupted." On the continent, this edition became the Textus Receptus or the Received Text. It seems that this success was in no small way due to the beauty and useful size of the Elzevir editions.

The Restoration Period

For the next 250 years, until 1881, textual scholarship was enslaved to the Erasmian-oriented Received Text. As these textual scholars[13] became familiar with older and more accurate manuscripts and observed the flaws in the Received Text, instead of changing the text, they would publish their findings in introductions, margins, and footnotes of their editions. In 1734, J. A. Bengel of Tübingen, Germany, made an apology for again printing the Received Text, doing so only "because he could not publish a text of his own. Neither the publisher nor the public would have stood for it," he complained. (Robertson 1925, 25)

The first one to break free from this enslavement to the Textus Receptus, in the text itself, was Bible scholar J. J. Griesbach (1745-1812). His principal edition comes to us in three volumes, the first in Halle in 1775-7, the second in Halle and London in 1796-1806, and the third at Leipzig in 1803-7. However, Griesbach did not fully break from the Textus Receptus. Nevertheless, Griesbach is the real starting point in the development of classifying the manuscripts into families, setting down principles and rules for establishing the original reading, and using symbols to indicate the degree of certainty as to its being the original reading. We will examine his contributions in more detail below.

Karl Lachmann (1793-1851) was the first scholar fully to get out from under the influence of the Textus Receptus. He was a professor of ancient classical languages at Berlin University. In 1831, he published his edition of the Greek New Testament without any regard to the Textus Receptus. As Samuel MacAuley Jackson expressed it: Lachmann "was the first to found a text wholly on ancient evidence; and his editions, to which his eminent reputation as a critic gave wide currency, especially in Germany, did much toward breaking down the superstitious reverence for the textus receptus." Bruce Metzger had harsh words for the era of the Textus Receptus as well:

So superstitious has been the reverence accorded the Textus Receptus that in some cases attempts to criticize it or emend it have been regarded as akin to sacrilege. Yet its textual basis is essentially a handful of late and haphazardly collected minuscule

---

[13] Brian Walton (1600-61), Dr. John Fell (1625-86), John Mill 1645-1707), Dr. Edward Wells (1667-1727, Richard Bentley (1662-1742), John Albert Bengel (1687-1752), Johann Jacob Wettstein (1693-1754), Johann Salomo Semler (1725-91), William Bowyer Jr. (1699-1777), Edward Harwood (1729-94), and Isaiah Thomas Jr. (1749-1831)

manuscripts, and in a dozen passages its reading is supported by no known Greek witnesses. (B. M. Metzger 1964, 1968, 1992, 106)

Subsequent to Lachmann came Friedrich Constantine von Tischendorf (1815-74), best known for his discovery of the famed fourth-century Codex Sinaiticus manuscript, the only Greek uncial manuscript containing the complete Greek New Testament. Tischendorf went further than any other textual scholar to edit and made accessible the evidence contained in leading as well as less important uncial manuscripts. Throughout the time that Tischendorf was making his valuable contributions to the field of textual criticism in Germany, another great scholar, Samuel Prideaux Tregelles (1813-75) in England made other valued contributions. Among them, he was able to establish his concept of "Comparative Criticism." That is, the age of a text, such as Vaticanus 1209, may not necessarily be that of its manuscript (i.e. the material upon which the text was written), which was copied in 350 C.E., since the text may be a faithful copy of an earlier text, like the second-century P[75]. Both Tischendorf and Tregelles were determined defenders of divine inspiration of the Scriptures, which likely had much to do with the productivity of their labors. If you take an opportunity to read about the lengths to which Tischendorf went in his discovery of Codex Sinaiticus, you will be moved by his steadfastness and love for God's Word.

The Climax of the Restored Text

The critical text of Westcott and Hort of 1881 has been commended by many leading textual scholars over the last one hundred and forty years, and still stands as the standard. Numerous additional critical editions of the Greek text came after Westcott and Hort: Richard F. Weymouth (1886), Bernhard Weiss (1894–1900); the British and Foreign Bible Society (1904, 1958), Alexander Souter (1910), Hermann von Soden (1911–1913); and Eberhard Nestle's Greek text, *Novum Testamentum Graece*, published in 1898 by the Württemberg Bible Society, Stuttgart, Germany. The Nestle in twelve editions (1898–1923) to subsequently be taken over by his son, Erwin Nestle (13th–20th editions, 1927–1950), followed by Kurt Aland (21st–25th editions, 1952–1963), and lastly, it was coedited by Kurt Aland and Barbara Aland (26th–27th editions, 1979–1993), and recently, the (28th edition, 2012).

Bruce M. Metzger explains the immense impact that the critical text of Westcott and Hort,

It was the corrupt Byzantine form of text that provided the basis for almost all translations of the New Testament into modern languages down to the nineteenth century. During the eighteenth century scholars assembled a great amount of information from many Greek manuscripts, as well as from versional and patristic witnesses. But, except for three or four editors who timidly corrected some of the more blatant errors of the Textus Receptus, this debased form of the New Testament text was reprinted in edition after edition. It was only in the first part of the nineteenth century (1831) that a German classical scholar, Karl Lachmann, ventured to apply to the New Testament the criteria that he had used in editing texts of the classics. Subsequently, other critical editions appeared, including those prepared by Constantin von Tischendorf, whose eighth edition (1869–72) remains a monumental thesaurus of variant readings, and the **influential edition prepared by two Cambridge scholars, B. F. Westcott and F. J. A. Hort (1881)**. It is the latter edition that was taken as **the basis for the present United Bible Societies' edition**. During the twentieth century, with the discovery of several New Testament manuscripts much older than any that had hitherto been available, it has become possible to produce editions of the New Testament that approximate ever more closely to what is regarded as the wording of the original documents.—Bruce Manning Metzger, United Bible Societies, A Textual Commentary on the Greek New Testament, Second Edition a Companion Volume to the United Bible Societies' Greek New Testament (4th Rev. Ed.) (London; New York: United Bible Societies, 1994), xxiv.

Many of the above scholars gave their entire lives to God and the Greek text. Each of these could have an entire book devoted to them and their work alone. The amount of work they accomplished before the era of computers is nothing short of astonishing. Rightly, the preceding history should serve to strengthen our faith in the authenticity and general integrity of the Greek New Testament. Unlike Bart D. Ehrman, men like Sir Frederic Kenyon have been moved to say that the books of the Greek New Testament have "come down to us substantially as they were written." And all this is especially true of the critical scholarship of the almost two hundred years since the days of Karl Lachmann, due to which all today can feel certain that what they hold in their hands is a mirror reflection of the Word of God that was penned in twenty-seven books, some two thousand years ago.

CHAPTER 2 Why Have Modern Bible Translations Removed Words, Phrases, Sentences, Even Whole Verses?

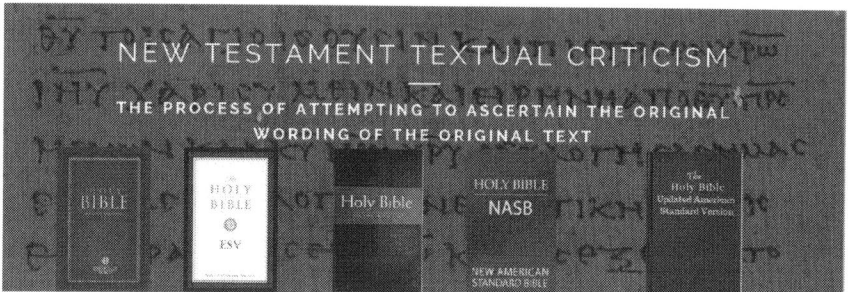

As some Christians have been studying their King James Version and comparing it to other modern translations, they have discovered that in the King James Version there are verses that these other translators removed, such as our Luke 17:36 under discussion herein, as well as Matthew 18:11; 23:14 that we discussed earlier this week, and others. Many uninformed or willfully blind King James Onlyist have used these verses to misinform readers of the King James Version. Below will be a detailed reason why they are missing from the modern Bible translations, except the Holman Christian Standard Bible and the New American Standard Bible. Thereafter, we will offer more technical internal and external evidence as to why.

The Warning from God

Deuteronomy 4:2; 12:32 Updated American Standard Version (UASV)

[2] You shall not add to the word which I am commanding you, nor take away from it, that you may keep the commandments of Jehovah your God which I command you. [32] "Everything that I command you, you shall be careful to do; you shall not add to nor take away from it.

Revelation 22:18-19 Updated American Standard Version (UASV)

[18] I testify to everyone who hears the words of the prophecy of this book: if anyone adds to them, God will add to him the plagues which are written in this book; [19] and if anyone takes away from the words of the book of this prophecy, God will take away his part from the tree of life and out of the holy city, which are written in this book.

Copying Manuscripts

Some are still not aware that no Bible translator has had access to the originals of the New Testament when making their translations because they have not been in existence for almost 2,000 years. Even if they were discovered, we could never ascertain that they were the originals unless they were autographed by Matthew, Mark, Luke, John, James, Peter, or Jude. Almost immediately after the originals were written, copies were being made to be used by the early Christian church.

We have inherited from the past generation the view that the early text was a 'free' text, and the discovery of the Chester Beatty papyri seemed to confirm this view. When P^{45} and P^{46} were joined by P^{66} sharing the same characteristics, this position seemed to be definitely established. P^{75} appeared in contrast to be a loner with its "strict" text anticipating Codex Vaticanus. Meanwhile, the other witnesses of the early period had been ignored. It is their collations which have changed the picture so completely.[14]

While we have said this once, it bears repeating, as *some* of the earliest manuscripts that we now have evidence that a professional scribe copied them. *Many* of the other papyri confirm that a semiprofessional hand copied them, while *most* of these early papyri give evidence of being produced by a copyist who was literate and experienced. Therefore, either literate or semiprofessional copyist did the vast majority of the early extant papyri, with some being done by professionals. As it happened, the few poorly copied manuscripts became known first, establishing a precedent that was difficult for some to shake when the enormous amount of evidence emerged that showed just the opposite.

The most reliable of the earliest texts are P^1, $P^{4, 64, 67}$, P^{23}, P^{27}, P^{30}, P^{32}, P^{35}, $P^{39, P49, 65}$, P^{70}, P^{75}, P^{86}, P^{87}, P^{90}, P^{91}, P^{100}, P^{101}, P^{106}, P^{108}, P^{111}, P^{114}, and P^{115}. The copyists of these manuscripts allowed very few variants in their copies of the exemplars. They had the ability to make accurate judgments as they went about their copying, resulting in superior texts. Whether their skills in copying were a result of their belief that they were copying a sacred text, or from their training, cannot be known. It could have been a combination of both. These papyri are of great importance when considering textual problems and are considered by many textual scholars to be a good representation of the original wording of the text that was first published by the biblical author. Still, "many of these manuscripts contain singular readings and some 'Alexandrian' polishing, which needs to be sifted out."

---

[14] (Aland and Aland, The Text of the New Testament 1995, 93-5)

30

(P. Comfort 2005, 269) Nevertheless, again, they are the best texts and the most faithful in preserving the original. While it is true that some of the papyri are mere fragments, some contain substantial portions of text. We should note too that text types really did not exist per se in the second century, and it is a mere convention to refer to the papyri as Alexandrian, since the best Alexandrian manuscript, Vaticanus, did exist in the second century by way of P[75]. It is not that the Alexandrian text existed, but rather P[75]/Vaticanus evidence that some very strict copying with great care was taking place. Manuscripts that were not of this caliber of strict and careful copying were the result of scribal errors and scribes taking liberties with the text. Therefore, even though P[5] may be categorized as a Western text-type, it is more a matter of negligence in the copying process.

"What we do know, from the manuscript evidence, is that several of the earliest Christian scribes were well-trained scribes who applied their training to making reliable texts, both of the Old Testament and the New Testament. We know that they were conscientious to make a reliable text in the process of transcription (as can been seen in manuscripts like P[4+64+67] and P[75]), and we know that others worked to rid the manuscript of textual corruption. This is nowhere better manifested than in P[66], where the scribe himself and the *diorthotes* (official corrector) made over 450 corrections to the text of John. As is explained in the next chapter, the *diorthotes* of P[66] probably consulted other exemplars (one whose text was much like that of P[75]) in making his corrections. This shows a standard Alexandrian scriptoral practice at work in the reproduction of a New Testament manuscript." (P. Comfort, Encountering the Manuscripts: An Introduction to New Testament Paleography and Textual Criticism 2005, 264)

While we can say that the early Alexandrian copyists certainly made some mistakes at times and added some intentional changes, generally, they used extreme care to make certain that their work was an exact duplication of the exemplar (archetype; master copy) that they were copying. Metzger tells us of another family of manuscripts, "The *Byzantine text*, otherwise called the *Syrian text* (so Westcott and Hort), ..., on the whole, the latest of the several distinctive types of text of the New Testament. It is characterized chiefly by lucidity and completeness. The framers of this text sought to smooth away any harshness of language, to combine two or more divergent readings into one expanded reading (called conflation), and to harmonize divergent parallel passages. This conflated text, produced perhaps at Antioch in Syria, was taken to Constantinople, whence it was distributed widely throughout the Byzantine Empire."[15]

It went something like this, a scribe who was very familiar with the Gospel of Matthew, as he is going about the work of copying the Gospel of Mark or Luke, tended to pen the wording that he had memorized from Matthew. Another way these interpolations crept into the text was carried out unintentionally as well. The scribe who is familiar with the Gospels may take note that a sentence that Matthew used was not to be found in Mark or Luke, so the scribe decides to add the sentence into the margin. However, a later copyist using this manuscript as his exemplar might not know if the sentence that has been added to the margin is there because it should be in the main text, so he moves the sentence from the margin to the main text in his copy of Mark or Luke, as it makes the accounts agree more closely. For example, In Luke's account of the Lord's Prayer, some manuscripts (A C D W Θ Ψ 070 f[13] 33[vid] Maj it syr[c,h,p]cop) add "Our Father who is in heaven"[16] (Luke 11:2a) Also, in Luke 11:2b, which should read "let your kingdom come," some manuscripts (D it[d]) expand it to, "let your kingdom come upon us."[17] In addition, in Luke 11:2c, some manuscripts (א A C D W Θ Ψ 070 f 33 Maj it syr[.p] cop[bo]) add "let your will be done on earth as it is in heaven," which is not present in (P[75] B L syr[c.] Marcion Origen).[18] The weightier manuscript evidence suggests that this interpolation was taken from Matthew 6:10. These harmonizations were interpolations from sincerely motivated scribes with good intentions.

Why should this brief history of our Greek New Testament be so important to us? How can our knowing that Erasmus created the first printed master Greek text with chiefly two corrupt twelfth-century manuscripts help us today, some 500 years after 1516? The reason that it is important to us is because of the impact Erasmus' master Greek text had.

The fact that Erasmus was terribly rushed resulted in a Greek text that contained hundreds of typographical errors alone.[19] Textual scholar Scrivener once stated: '[It] is in that respect the most faulty book I know'

---

[15] Bruce Manning Metzger, United Bible Societies, *A Textual Commentary on the Greek New Testament, Second Edition a Companion Volume to the United Bible Societies' Greek New Testament (4th Rev. Ed.)* (London; New York: United Bible Societies, 1994), xxi.

[16] Philip W. Comfort, *New Testament Text and Translation Commentary: Commentary on the Variant Readings of the Ancient New Testament Manuscripts and How They Relate to the Major English Translations* (Carol Stream, IL: Tyndale House Publishers, Inc., 2008), 202.

[17] IBID., 202.

[18] IBID., 203.

[19] In fact, his copy of Revelation being incomplete, Erasmus simply retranslated the missing verses from the Latin Vulgate back into Greek.

(Scrivener 1894, 185). This comment did not even take into consideration the blatant interpolations into the text that were not part of the original. Sir Frederic Kenyon made this observation about the Textus Receptus, "The result is that the text accepted in the sixteenth and seventeenth centuries, to which we have clung from a natural reluctance to change the words which we have learnt as those of the Word of God, is in truth full of inaccuracies, many of which can be corrected with absolute certainty from the vastly wider information which is at our disposal today."[20] Erasmus was not oblivious to the typographical errors, which were corrected in a good many later editions. This did not include the textual errors. It was his second edition of 1519 that was used by Martin Luther in his German translation and William Tyndale's English translation.

Even though dozens of others had given their lives to the restoration of the Greek New Testament text, the pinnacle of those efforts came in the late 19th century with B. F. Westcott and F. J. A. Hort, who produced a restored text in 1881 that has been widely accepted. Westcott and Hort carried out their work so meticulously and thoroughly, possessing such knowledge insight, and skill that all textual scholars since then have been working in reaction to their work. This restored text of Westcott and Hort has been the basis for almost all modern-day translations. On this Metzger writes,

> Subsequently, other critical editions appeared, including those prepared by Constantin von Tischendorf, whose eighth edition (1869–72) remains a monumental thesaurus of variant readings, and the influential edition prepared by two Cambridge scholars, B. F. Westcott and F. J. A. Hort (1881). **It is the latter edition that was taken as the basis for the present United Bible Societies' edition.** During the twentieth century, with the discovery of several New Testament manuscripts much older than any that had hitherto been available, it has become possible to produce editions of the New Testament that approximate ever more closely to what is regarded as the wording of the original documents.[21] (Bold mine)

---

[20] Frederic G. Kenyon Sr., Our Bible and the Ancient Manuscripts: Being a History of the Text and Its Translations (London: Eyre & Spottiswood, 1896), 162.

[21] Bruce Manning Metzger, United Bible Societies, A Textual Commentary on the Greek New Testament, Second Edition a Companion Volume to the United Bible Societies' Greek New Testament (4th Rev. Ed.) (London; New York: United Bible Societies, 1994), xxiv.

Some Verses That Should Not Have Ever Been

Matthew 17:21 King James Version (KJV)	Matthew 17:21 Updated American Standard Version (UASV)
21 Howbeit this kind goeth not out but by prayer and fasting.	21 ——

Many later Greek manuscripts add vs 21, scribes making it agree with Mark 9:29, [But this kind does not go out except by prayer and fasting.] However, the earliest, weightiest, and diverse manuscripts ℵ* B Θ 0281 33 892* itᵉ Syᶜ,ˢ copˢᵃ WHNU does not contain vs 21.

Matthew 18:11 King James Version (KJV)	Matthew 18:11 Updated American Standard Version (UASV)
11 For the Son of man is come to save that which was lost.	11 ——

The earliest and most trusted two manuscripts (ℵ B) do not include variant 1 or variant 2. Also excluding these variants is L* Θ* f¹, 33 itᵉ syrˢ copˢᵃ Origen as well. Multiple later manuscripts (D L W Θᶜ 078 Maj syrᶜ,ᵖ) ad variant 1: "For the Son of Man has come to save that which was lost." Several other manuscripts (Lᵐᵍ 892ᶜ itᶜ syrʰ) would expand upon this reading in variant 2: "For the Son of Man came to seek and to save the lost." Based on their not being in the most important and trusted witnesses and diverse witnesses (Alexandrian, Egyptian, Antiochian), clearly, variant 1 and variant 2 are interpolations (spurious) were not part of the original. It seems that the copyists inserted this verse in the text to create some sort of bridge between Matthew 18:10 and 18:12, so they borrowed it from Luke 19:10, which is not even parallel to this one. In all likelihood, the shorter variant came first, and a later copyist expanded upon it with the longer variant 2, bringing it to the point where it corresponds exactly with Luke 19:10.

Matthew 23:14 King James Version (KJV)	Matthew 23:14 Updated American Standard Version (UASV)
14 Woe unto you, scribes and Pharisees, hypocrites! for ye devour widows' houses, and for a pretence make long prayer: therefore ye shall receive the greater damnation.	14 ——

This verse was taken from Mark 12:40 or Luke 20:47 and inserted **before** verse 13 of Matthew Chapter 24 in the *Majority Text* (W 0102 0107 it syr^h,p) but **after** verse 13 in the *Textus Receptus* (f^13 it syr^c). It was not in the original text of Matthew per it not being in the early weighty documentary witnesses against the reading from the Alexandrian and Western text types. (א B D L Z Θ f^1 33 it^e syr^s cop^sa) This type of harmonization of the gospels was common after the fourth century CE and is characteristic of the Byzantine text-type. Both the KJV and the NKJV part company with the Textus Receptus and instead went with the Majority Text when they placed the verse after verse 13. Many modern-day translations cite the verse in a footnote out of respect for its long history in the English Bible. The HCSB and the NASB take it to the next level out of reverence for the KJV and the NKJV readers, so they place this interpolation right in the main text within square brackets with footnotes that read, "Other MSS omit bracketed text" and "This v not found in early mss" respectively. However, it should be noted that the 2017 CSB removed this spurious verse from the main text. The HCSB and the NASB are not helping their readers by clinging to a translation that is based on corrupt, inferior manuscripts support.

Mark 7:16 King James Version (KJV)	Mark 7:16 Updated American Standard Version (UASV)
16 If any man have ears to hear, let him hear.	16 ——

WH NU א B L Δ* 0274 al omit; A D W Θ f^.13 33 Maj, "If anyone has ears to hear, let him hear." The scribe clearly added this verse from 4:9 or 4:23, as it is nearly identical, possibly seeking to provide an ending for a short pericope.

Mark 9:44, 46 King James Version (KJV)	Mark 9:44, 46 Updated American Standard Version (UASV)
44 Where their worm dieth not, and the fire is not quenched. 46 Where their worm dieth not, and the fire is not quenched.	44 —— 46 ——

WH NU א B C L W ΔΨ 0274 f^1 28 565 it^k syr^s cop omit; A D Θ f^13 Maj, "where their worm does not die and the fire is not quenched." This verse is identical to verse 48 and is missing from the earliest and best manuscripts, as well as several text types. It is an interpolation.

WH NU א B C L W ΔΨ 0274 f¹ 28 565 itᵏ syrˢ cop omit; A D Θ f¹³ Maj, "where their worm does not die and the fire is not quenched." This verse is identical to verse 48 and is missing from the earliest and best manuscripts, as well as several text types. It is an interpolation.

Mark 11:26 King James Version (KJV)	Mark 11:26 Updated American Standard Version (UASV)
26 But if ye do not forgive, neither will your Father which is in heaven forgive your trespasses.	26 ——

Many later Greek manuscripts added vs 26, as the scribes were expanding on verse 25, inserting the words from Matt. 6:15 making it agree with its parallel account. [But if you do not forgive, neither will your Father who is in the heavens forgive your trespasses.] However, the omission has much stronger manuscript support: א B L W Δ Ψ 565 700 syrˢ WH NU omit vs 26.

Mark 15:28 King James Version (KJV)	Mark 15:28 Updated American Standard Version (UASV)
28 And the scripture was fulfilled, which saith, And he was numbered with the transgressors.	28 ——

WH NU omit verse, which is supported by the earliest and best manuscripts א A B C D Ψ itᵏ syrˢ copˢᵃ. A variant/TR add verse Και επληρωθη η γραφη η λεγουσα· και μετα ανομων ελογισθη "And the Scripture was fulfilled that says, 'He was counted among the lawless,'" which is supported by L Θ 083 0250 f¹·¹³ Maj syrʰ·ᵖ.

Luke 17:36 King James Version (KJV)	Luke 17:36 Updated American Standard Version (UASV)
36 Two men shall be in the field; the one shall be taken, and the other left.	36——

The earliest and most reliable manuscripts (P⁷⁵ א A B L W Δ Θ Ψ f¹ 33 cop·ᵇᵒ) does not contain 17:36, while later manuscripts (D f 700 it syr) does contain verse 36, "Two men will be in the field; one will be taken and the other will be left." This is likely a scribal interpolation taken from Matthew 24:40. This verse is missing from Tyndale's version (1534) and the Geneva Bible (1557). Even the King James Version translators had their doubts about 17:36, as it reads in the original 1611 edition and a sidenote in good quality editions today, "This 36th verse is wanting in most of the Greek copies."

John 5:3b-4 King James Version (KJV)	John 5:3b-4 Updated American Standard Version (UASV)
[3] In these lay a great multitude of impotent folk, of blind, halt, withered, waiting for the moving of the water. [4] For an angel went down at a certain season into the pool, and troubled the water: whosoever then first after the troubling of the water stepped in was made whole of whatsoever disease he had.	[3] In these lay a multitude of sick ones, blind, lame, and paralyzed. [4]———

The earliest and best witnesses (P[66] P[75] ℵ B C D L T W[s] 33 579 1241 it sy[c] co) **do not have** John 5:3b-4 in their exemplar; Other later witnesses (A[c] C[3] D K W[s] Γ Δ Θ Ψ 078 $f^{1.13}$ 33. 565. 579. 700. 892. 1241. 1424 Maj lat sy[p.h] bo[pt]) did contain: "waiting for the moving of the water. [4] For an angel of the Lord would come down at certain seasons into the pool and stirred the water. Whoever went in first after the stirring of the water was healed of whatever disease he had." This interpolation was added by later scribes to explain the sick man's answer in verses 7 where he describes 'the water being stirred up.'

Acts 8:37 King James Version (KJV)	Acts 8:37 Updated American Standard Version (UASV)
[37] And Philip said, If thou believest with all thine heart, thou mayest. And he answered and said, I believe that Jesus Christ is the Son of God.	[37]———

The earliest and best Greek manuscripts (P[45, 74] ℵ A B C) as well as 33 81 614 vg syr[p.h] cop[sa.bo]eth Chrysostom Ambrose do not contain vs 37, while other manuscripts 4[mg] (E 1739 it syr[h**] Irenaeus Cyprian) contain, And Philip said, "If you believe with all your heart, you may." And he replied, "I believe that Jesus Christ is the Son of God." If this were apart of the original, there is no good reason why it would be missing in so many early witnesses and versions. This is a classic example of a scribe taking liberties with the text by answering the Eunuch's question ("Look! Water! What prevents me from being baptized?") with ancient Christian baptismal practices from a later age.

Acts 15:34 King James Version (KJV)	Acts 15:34 Updated American Standard Version (UASV)
34 Notwithstanding it pleased Silas to abide there still.	34——

Verse 34 is not contained in the earliest and diverse manuscripts (P[74] א A B E Ψ Maj syr[p] cop[bo]), while vs 34 is contained in two different forms in other manuscripts (C 33 614 1739 syr** cop[sa]) "But it seemed good to Silas to remain there" and (P[127vid] D it.[w]) "But it seemed good to Silas to remain with them, so Judas traveled alone." The scribes likely incorporated a gloss from the margin that was trying to rationalize why Silas just happened to be there in verse 40 for the apostle Paul to choose him as a traveling companion. The only problem is that the interpolation of vs 34 contradicts vs 33.

Acts 24:6b–8a King James Version (KJV)	Acts 24:6b–8a Updated American Standard Version (UASV)
6 Who also hath gone about to profane the temple: whom we took, and would have judged according to our law. 7 But the chief captain Lysias came upon us, and with great violence took him away out of our hands, 8 Commanding his accusers to come unto thee: by examining of whom thyself mayest take knowledge of all these things, whereof we accuse him.	6 He even tried to desecrate the temple, but we seized him. 7 —— 8 When you examine him yourself, you will find out about all these things of which we are accusing him."

P[74] א A B H L P 049 cop omit the following from vss 6-8, which read, according to (E) Ψ Maj 33 614 1739 it (syr): "We wanted to judge him according to our own Law. 7 But Lysias the commander came along, and with much violence took him out of our hands, 8 ordering his accusers to come before you." The earliest and most reliable manuscripts have the shorter reading. The interpolation is a classic example of a scribe trying to fill in what he perceives to be gaps in the text.

Acts 28:29 King James Version (KJV)	Acts 28:29 Updated American Standard Version (UASV)
29 And when he had said these words, the Jews departed, and had great reasoning among themselves.	29 ——

The earliest and best Greek manuscripts (P⁷⁴ ℵ A B E Ψ 048 33 1739 syrᵖ cop) do not contain vs 29, while is later less trusted manuscripts (Maj it syrʰ**) that contain Acts 28:29, "When he had spoken these words, the Jews departed, having a great dispute among themselves." This is another example of later scribes seeking to fill in the narrative where they perceive there is a gap in the account.

Romans 16:24 King James Version (KJV)	Romans 16:24 Updated American Standard Version (UASV)
24 The grace of our Lord Jesus Christ be with you all. Amen.	24 ——

The earliest and best manuscripts (P⁴⁶ P⁶¹ ℵ A B C 1739 Itᵇ cop) do not contain vs 24, while later witnesses (D Ψ Maj syrʰ) contain 16:24, "The grace of our Lord Jesus Christ be with you all. Amen," with F G omitting Ιησου Χριστου [Jesus Christ]. This verse is the same as the end of vs 20. All modern translations do not include this verse because of the superior testimony against it.

1 John 5:7-8 King James Version (KJV)	1 John 5:7-8 Updated American Standard Version (UASV)
7 For there are three that bear record in heaven, the Father, the Word, and the Holy Ghost: and these three are one. 8 And there are three that bear witness in earth, the Spirit, and the water, and the blood: and these three agree in one.	7 For there are three that testify: 8 the Spirit and the water and the blood; and the three are in agreement.

The earliest and best manuscripts (ℵ A B (Ψ) Maj syr cop arm eth it) do not contain this spurious interpolation. Only eight late Greek manuscripts add "… in heaven, the Father, the Word, and the Holy Spirit, and these three are one. 8 And there are three that testify on earth, the Spirit." If this passage had been in the original, there is no good reason why

39

it would have been removed either accidentally or intentionally. None of the Greek church fathers quote this passage, which they certainly would have during the Trinitarian controversy. (Sabellian and Arian). This interpolation is not in any of the ancient versions, such as Syriac, Coptic, Armenian, Ethiopic, Arabic, Slavonic, and the Old Latin in its early form, or Jerome's Latin Vulgate. Intrinsically, the interpolation "makes an awkward break in the sense" as Metzger points out.

Some other verses that contain interpolations (italics is the spurious portion) are **Matthew 20:16** (*b*) KJV: [16] ... *for many be called, but few chosen.* **Mark 6:11** (*b*) KJV: [11] And whosoever shall not receive you, nor hear you, when ye depart thence, shake off the dust under your feet, for a testimony against them: *Verily I say unto you, it shall be more tolerable for Sodom and Gomorrah in the Day of Judgement, than for that city.* [12] And they went out, and preached ... **Luke 4:8** (*b*) KJV: [8]And Jesus answered and said unto to him [the Devil], "*Get thee behind me, Satan, for* it is written, ..." **Luke 23:17** KJV: *For of necessity he must release one unto them at the feast.* Acts 9:5-6 KJV: [5] And he [Paul] said, 'Who art thou Lord?' and the Lord said, 'I am Jesus whom thou persecutest. *It is hard for thee to kick against the pricks.'* [6] *And he, trembling and astonished, said, 'Lord, what wilt thou have me to do?' And the Lord said unto him,* 'Arise, and go into the city, and it shall be told thee what thou must do.'

As was mentioned above, some scribes have added a sentence or even an entire verse from elsewhere to another part of the manuscript he was copying. This is clearly made evident in Mark 9:43-48. In the above Bible translations, you can see that verses 44 and 46 are omitted in the main text with the omission noted in the footnote. The only exception in the NASB and the HCSB, which bracketed 44 and 46 in the main text. These translation committees and most biblical scholars today believe verses 44 and 46 were not part of the original text. It could be the translation committees are clinging to the King James Version readers. The text of verses 44 and 46 reads, "where their worm does not die, and the fire is not quenched," the same as in verse 48.

Mark 9:44: WH NU א B C L W ΔΨ 0274 f[1] 28 565 it[k] syr[s] cop omit; A D Θ f[13] Maj, "where their worm does not die and the fire is not quenched." This verse is identical to verse 48 and is missing from the earliest and best manuscripts, as well as several text types. It is an interpolation.

Mark 9:46: WH NU א B C L W ΔΨ 0274 f[1] 28 565 it[k] syr[s] cop omit; A D Θ f[13] Maj, "where their worm does not die and the fire is not quenched." This verse is identical to verse 48 and is missing from the earliest and best manuscripts, as well as several text types. It is an interpolation.

Clearly, as the evidence suggests a scribe or scribes simply repeated verse 48. This could have been intentional or unintentional. Therefore, when modern translations remove verse 44 and 46; they are not removing part of God's Word because (1) it was never a part of God's Word in the first place and (2) the same sentence is right there in verse 48 of the same account. However, what are these translations accomplishing by removing these two spurious interpolations? The text is being restored to what Mark had been inspired to write.

Looking again at our example verse above, we note that there are other cases where the verses come not from the same book but from another book of the Bible. There are generally footnotes that help the reader to see this but often, the translations do not give the reader enough information so he or she can fully understand. If you compare your King James Version with the modern translations, you will discover that the verse that has been omitted, it is merely a verse repeated from another place in that book or another Bible book. If we look at Romans 16:24 again, we will see that the earliest and best manuscripts (P⁴⁶ P⁶¹ ℵ A B C 1739 It^b cop) do not contain vs 24, while later witnesses (D Ψ Maj syr^h) contain 16:24, "The grace of our Lord Jesus Christ be with you all. Amen," with F G omitting Ιησου Χριστου [Jesus Christ]. This verse is the same as the end of vs 20. All modern translations do not include this verse because of the superior testimony against it. When we compare 16:24 with 16:20 and the closing passages in almost any of the books written by the apostle Paul, we discover that at Romans 16:24, some scribe plainly added a closing expression that is identical to or very similar to the conclusion in almost all of Paul's books.

Trusting the Greek New Testament

As we have looked at a few verses that obviously were not part of the original inspired text that the author penned, this should not leave us doubting the trustworthiness of God's Word. We should not forget that 90% of the Hebrew Old Testament Text is without significant variation and 93% of the Greek New Testament Text is without significant variation. We have the work of hundreds of textual scholars from the days of Desiderius Erasmus, who have given their entire lives to the restoration of the Greek New Testament. Therefore, textual scholars only need to focus their attention on this tiny 07% of significant textual variants. These variants that have been corrected have not undermined the Word of God, instead they highlight and stress the fact that God has preserved his Word through restoration.

CHAPTER 3 Do We Need the Original Bible Manuscripts?

Between 3,500 years ago and 2,460 years ago some 32+ authors penned 39 books in the Middle East, compiling a history of the world from its creation, to the flood of Noah, the confusing of the languages at Babylon, Abraham entering Canaan, to the formation of the Israelite nation, to the rise and fall of the Egyptian, Assyrian, Babylonian, Medo-Persian Empires. These 39 books became the most important collection of literature that the world has ever known. They would soon be joined by another 27 books, the second most important collection that was written some 2,000 years ago, covering the birth of the Roman Empire and the birth of the Son of God, as well as the birth and foundation of Christianity.

There was something different about this library of sixty-six books that had been penned over a 1600-year period. The authors came from every walk of life from lowly fisherman and shepherds to a military general, a physician, a tax collector, kings, and the like. These 40+ men were moved along by the Holy Spirit so that what they produced was not theirs alone but belonged to one author, the Creator of all thing, God himself. This means that these sixty-six books possessed perfect content (fully inerrant/infallible) with no errors, mistakes, contradictions. We still have translations of these writings today that can be read by almost everyone on earth. However, a question arises because the copyists who were making copies for thousands of years were not moved along by the Holy Spirit. We do not have the original manuscripts. We know that the thousands upon thousands of original language manuscripts (Hebrew OT/Greek NT) and the versions all read differently, as there are hundreds of thousands of scribal errors. How can we be sure that what we have in our Bible translations is really an accurate translation of what the authors originally wrote?

How Our Bible Manuscripts Survived the Elements

One may wonder why more Old and New Testament manuscripts have not survived. Really, the better question would be how come so many of our Bible manuscripts survived in comparison to ancient secular manuscripts? The primary materials used to receive writing in ancient times were perishable papyrus and parchment. It must be remembered that the Christians suffered intense persecution during intervals in the first 300 years from Pentecost 33 C.E. With this persecution from the Roman Empire came many orders to destroy Christian texts. In addition, these texts were not stored in such a way as to secure their preservation; they were actively used by the Christians in the congregation and were subject to wear and tear.

Furthermore, moisture is the enemy of papyrus, and it causes them to disintegrate over time. This is why, as we will discover, the papyrus manuscripts that have survived have come from the dry sands of Egypt. Moreover, it seems not to have entered the minds of the early Christians to preserve their documents, because their solution to the loss of manuscripts was just to make more copies. Fortunately, the process of making copies transitioned to the more durable animal skins, which would last much longer. Those that have survived, especially from the fourth century C.E. and earlier, are the path to restoring the original Greek New Testament.[22]

Both papyrus and parchment jeopardized the survival of the Bible because they were perishable materials. Papyrus, the weakest of the two, can tear and discolor. Because of moist climates, a sheet of papyrus can decay to the point where it is nothing more than a handful of dust. We must remember papyrus is a plant and when the scroll has been stored, it can grow mold and it can rot from dampness. It can even be eaten by starving rodents or also insects, especially white ants (i.e., termites) when it has been buried. When some of the manuscripts were first discovered early on, they were exposed to excessive light and humidity, which hastened their deterioration.

While parchment is far more durable than papyrus, it will also perish in time if mishandled or exposed to the elements (temperature, humidity, and light) over time.[23] Parchment is made from animal skin, so it too is also

---

[22] Cf. J. H. Greenlee, *Introduction to New Testament Textual Criticism* (Peabody: Hendrickson, 1995), 11.

[23] For example, the official signed copy of the U.S. Declaration of Independence was written on parchment. Now, less than 250 years later, it has faded to the point of being barely legible.

a victim of insects. Hence, when it comes to ancient records, Everyday Writing in the Graeco-Roman East states, "survival is the exception rather than the rule." (R. S. Bagnall 2009, 140) Think about it for a moment; the Bible and its special revelation could have died from decay in the elements.

The Mosaic Law commanded every future king, "And when he sits on the throne of his kingdom, he shall write for himself in a book a copy of this law, approved by the Levitical priests." (Deuteronomy 17:18) Moreover, the professional copyist of the Hebrew Old Testament made so many manuscripts, by the time of Jesus and the apostles, throughout all of Israel and even into distant Macedonia, there were many copies of the Scriptures in the synagogues (Luke 4:16, 17; Acts 17:11) How did our Hebrew Old Testament and Greek New Testament survive the elements to the point where there are far more of them than any other ancient document. For example, there are 5,836 New Testament manuscripts in the original Greek alone.

New Testament scholar Philip W. Comfort writes, "Jews were known to put scrolls containing Scripture in pitchers or jars in order to preserve them. The Dead Sea scrolls found in jars in the Qumran caves are a celebrated example of this. The Beatty Papyri were very likely a part of a Christian library, which was hidden in jars to be preserved from confiscation during the Diocletian persecution."[24] Christianity were initially made up Jewish Christians only for the first seven years (29-36 C.E.), with Cornelius being the first Gentile baptized in 36 C.E. Much of early Christianity (33-350 C.E.) was made up of Jewish Christians, who evidently carried over the tradition of putting "scrolls containing Scripture in pitchers or jars in order to preserve them." It is for this reason that some of our earliest Bible manuscripts have been discovered in unusually dry regions, in clay jars and even dark closets and caves.

Manuscripts Saved from Egyptian Garbage Heaps

Beginning in 1778 and continuing to the end of the 19th century, many papyrus texts were accidentally discovered in Egypt that dated from 300 B.C.E. to 500 C.E., almost 500 million documents in all. About 130 years ago, there began a systematic search. At that time, a continuous flow of ancient texts was being found by the native fellahin, and the Egypt Exploration Society, a British non-profit organization, founded in 1882, realized that they needed to send out an expedition team before it was too late. They sent two Oxford scholars, Bernard P. Grenfell, and Arthur

---

[24] Philip Wesley Comfort and David P. Barrett, *The Text of the Earliest New Testament Greek Manuscripts* (Wheaton, IL: Tyndale House, 2001), 158.

S. Hunt, who received permission to search the area south of the farming region in the Faiyūm district. Grenfell chose a site called Behnesa because of its ancient Greek name, Oxyrhynchus. A search of the graveyards and the ruined houses produced nothing. The only place left to search was the town's garbage dumps, which were some 30 feet [9 m] high. It seems to Grenfell and Hunt that all was lost, but they decided to try.

In January of 1897, a trial trench (excavation or depression in the ground) was dug, and it only took a few hours before ancient papyrus materials were found. These included letters, contracts, and official documents. The sand had blown over them, covering them, and for nearly 2,000 years, the dry climate had served as a protection for them.

It took only a mere three months to pull out and recover almost two tons of papyri from Oxyrhynchus. They shipped twenty-five large cases back to England. Over the next ten years, these two courageous scholars returned each and every winter, to grow their collection. They discovered ancient classical writing, along with royal ordinances and contracts mixed in with business accounts private letters, shipping lists, as well as fragments of many New Testament manuscripts.

Of what benefit were all these documents? Foremost, the bulk of these documents were written by ordinary people in Koine (common) Greek of the day. Many of the words that would be used in the marketplace, not by the elites appeared in the Greek New Testament Scriptures, which woke scholars up to the fact that Biblical Greek was not some unique Greek, but instead, it was the ordinary language of the common people, the man on the street. Thus, by comparing how the words had been used in these papyri, a clearer understanding of Biblical Greek emerged. As of the time of this writing, less than ten percent of these papyri have been published and studied. Most of the papyri were found in the top 10 feet 93 m] of the garbage heap because the other 20 feet [6 m] had been ruined by water from a nearby canal. If we look at it simply, this would mean that the 500 thousand documents found could have been two million in total. Then, we must ponder just how many documents must have come through Oxyrhynchus that were never discarded in the dumps. We have almost a half-million papyrus documents (likely there were millions more that did not survive) in garbage dumps in the dry sands of Oxyrhynchus, Egypt.

The result is that the New Testament has been preserved in over **5,836** complete or fragmented Greek manuscripts, as well as some **10,000** Latin manuscripts and **9,300 manuscripts** in various other ancient languages, which include Syriac, Slavic, Gothic, Ethiopic, Coptic and Armenian. Some of these are well over 2,000 years old.

The Hebrew Scriptures ended up in the hands of the Masoretes (Mas·o·retes \ ˈma-sə-ˌrētes) scribe-scholars ('preservers of tradition') who worked between the 6th and 10th centuries C.E., based primarily in early medieval Palestine in the cities of Tiberias and Jerusalem. The Masoretes have not been adequately appreciated for their accomplishments. These nameless scribes copied the Hebrew Old Testament Scriptures with meticulous and loving care. As for the early Christian copyists of the New Testament, either literate or semi-professional copyist did the vast majority of the early papyri, with some being done by professionals.

It is true that the Jewish copyists, as well as the later Christian copyists, were not led along by the Holy Spirit and therefore their manuscripts were not inerrant, infallible. Errors (textual variants) crept into the manuscripts unintentionally and intentionally. However, the vast majority of the Hebrew Old Testament and Greek New Testament has not been infected with textual errors. For the portions impacted with textual errors, it is the many tens of thousands of copies that we have to help us to weed out the errors. How? Well, not every copyist made the same textual errors. Hence, by comparing the work of different copyists and different manuscripts, textual scholars, we can identify the textual variants (errors), remove those, which leaves us with the original content.

Yes, it would be the greatest discovery of all time if we found the actual original five books that were penned by Moses himself, Genesis through Deuteronomy. However, first, there would be no way of establishing that they were the originals. Second, truth be told, we do not need the originals. We do not need those original documents. What is so important about the documents? Nothing, it is the content on the original documents that we are after. And truly miraculously, we have more copies than needed to do just that. We do not need miraculous preservation because we have miraculous restoration. We now know beyond a reasonable doubt that the Greek New Testament critical text is a 99.5% reflection of the content that was in those ancient original manuscripts.

CHAPTER 4 How Did Our Bible Manuscripts Survive the Elements?

The Materials

The primary materials used to receive writing in ancient times was papyrus and parchment. These were used by Bible authors and copyists[25] as well. At 2 Timothy 4:13 the apostle Paul requested of Timothy that he "bring the cloak that I left with Carpus at Troas, also the books [scrolls], and above all the parchments [*membranas,* Greek spelling]." One might ask why Paul used a Latin word (transliterated in Greek)? Undoubtedly it was due to the fact that there was no Greek word that would serve as an equivalent to what he was requesting. It was only later that the transliterated "codex" was brought into the Greek language as a reference to what we would know as a book.

Papyrus: Papyrus was the writing material used by the ancient Egyptians, Greeks, and Romans that was made from the pith of the stem of a water plant. It was cut into strips, with one layer laid out horizontally and the other vertically. Sometimes it was covered with a cloth and then beaten with a mallet. Scholarship has also suggested that paste may have been used between layers, and then a large stone would be placed on top until the materials were dry.

---

[25] Papyrus is a writing material prepared in ancient Egypt from the pithy stem of a water plant, used in sheets throughout the ancient Mediterranean world for writing. Parchment is made from animal skins and was used as a durable writing surface in ancient times.

Writing on the papyrus sheet, even the correct side, was no easy task by any means because the surface was rough and fibrous. "Defects sometimes occurred in the making through retention of moisture between the layers or through the use of spongy strips which could cause ink to run; such flaws necessitated the remaking of the sheet." (Abbot, 1938, p. 11) The back pain from long periods of sitting cross-legged on the ground bent over a papyrus sheet on a board, dealing with running ink, the reed pen possibly snagging and tearing the papyrus sheet, having to erase illegible characters, all were a deterrent from personally writing a letter.

Animal Skin: About the fourth century C.E., Bible manuscripts made of papyrus began to be superseded by the use of vellum, a high-quality parchment made from calfskin, kidskin, or lambskin. Manuscripts such as the famous Codex Sinaiticus (01) and Codex Vaticanus (03, also known as B) of the fourth century C.E. are parchment, or vellum, codices. This use of parchment as the leading writing material continued for almost a thousand years until it was replaced by paper. The advantages of parchment over papyrus were many, such as (1) it was much easier to write on smooth parchment, (2) one could write on both sides, (3) parchment lasted much longer, and (4) when desired, old writing could be scraped off and the parchment reused.

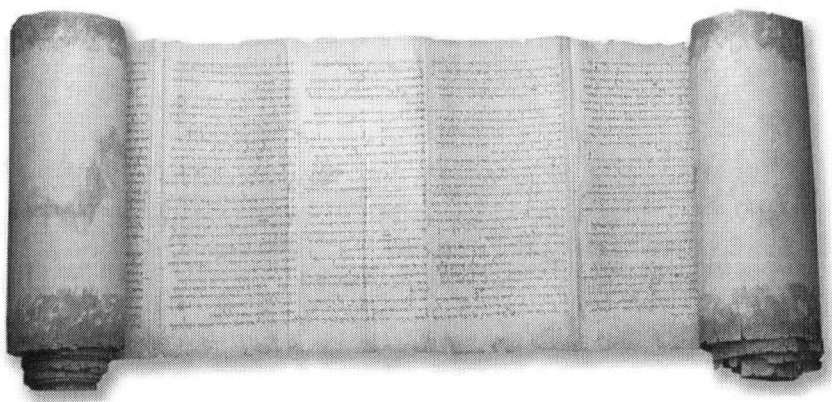

Image 1 A 2,000-year-old Dead Sea Isaiah Scroll. It matches closely the Masoretic text and what is in the Bible today

Danger from the Elements

One may wonder why more Old and New Testament manuscripts have not survived. It must be remembered that the Christians suffered intense persecution during intervals in the first 300 years from Pentecost 33 C.E. With this persecution from the Roman Empire came many orders to destroy Christian texts. In addition, these texts were not stored in such a way as to secure their preservation; they were actively used by the Christians in the congregation and were subject to wear and tear. Furthermore, moisture is the enemy of papyrus, and it causes them to disintegrate over time. This is why, as we will discover, the papyrus manuscripts that have survived have come from the dry sands of Egypt. Moreover, it seems not to have entered the minds of the early Christians to preserve their documents, because their solution to the loss of manuscripts was just to make more copies. Fortunately, the process of making copies transitioned to the more durable animal skins, which would last much longer. Those that have survived, especially from the fourth century C.E. and earlier, are the path to restoring the original Greek New Testament.[26]

Both papyrus and parchment jeopardized the survival of the Bible because they were perishable materials. **Papyrus,** the weakest of the two, can tear and discolor. Because of moist climates, a sheet of papyrus can decay to the point where it is nothing more than a handful of dust. We must remember papyrus is a plant, and when the scroll has been stored, it can grow mold, and it can rot from dampness. It can even be eaten by starving rodents or also insects, especially white ants (i.e., termites) when it has been buried. When some of the manuscripts were first discovered early on, they were exposed to excessive light and humidity, which hastened their deterioration.

While **parchment** is far more durable than papyrus, it will also perish in due course if mishandled or exposed to the elements (temperature, humidity, and light) over time.[27] Parchment is made from animal skin, so it too is also a victim of insects. Hence, when it comes to ancient records, *Everyday Writing in the Graeco-Roman East* states, "survival is the exception rather than the rule." (R. S. Bagnall 2009, 140) Think about it for a moment, the Bible and its special revelation could have died from decay in the elements.

How Did Our Bible Manuscripts Survive the Elements?

The Mosaic Law commanded every future king, "And when he sits on the throne of his kingdom, he shall write for himself in a book a copy of this law, approved by the Levitical priests." (Deuteronomy 17:18) Moreover, the professional copyist of the Hebrew Old Testament made so many manuscripts, by the time of Jesus and the apostles, throughout all of

---

[26] Cf. J. H. Greenlee, *Introduction to New Testament Textual Criticism* (Peabody: Hendrickson, 1995), 11.

[27] For example, the official signed copy of the U.S. Declaration of Independence was written on parchment. Now, less than 250 years later, it has faded to the point of being barely legible.

Israel and even into distant Macedonia, there were many copies of the Scriptures in the synagogues. (Luke 4:16, 17; Acts 17:11) How did our Hebrew Old Testament and Greek New Testament survive the elements to the point where there are far more of them than any other ancient document. For example, there are 5,836 New Testament manuscripts in the original Greek alone.

Image 2 Qumran Caves Where the Dead Sea Scrolls Were Found in 1947

New Testament scholar Philip W. Comfort writes, "Jews were known to put scrolls containing Scripture in pitchers or jars in order to preserve them. The Dead Sea scrolls found in jars in the Qumran caves are a celebrated example of this. The Beatty Papyri were very likely a part of a Christian library, which was hidden in jars to be preserved from confiscation during the Diocletian persecution."[28] Christianity were initially made up Jewish Christians only for the first seven years (29-36 C.E.), with Cornelius being the first Gentile baptized in 36 C.E. Much of early Christianity (33-350 C.E.) was made up of Jewish Christians, who evidently carried over the tradition of putting "scrolls containing Scripture in pitchers or jars in order to preserve them." It is for this reason that some of our earliest Bible manuscripts have been discovered in unusually dry regions, in clay jars and even dark closets and caves.

---

[28] Philip Wesley Comfort and David P. Barrett, *The Text of the Earliest New Testament Greek Manuscripts* (Wheaton, IL: Tyndale House, 2001), 158.

Manuscripts Saved from Egyptian Garbage Heaps

Beginning in 1778 and continuing to the end of the 19th century, many papyrus texts were accidentally discovered in Egypt that dated from 300 B.C.E. to 500 C.E., almost 500 million documents in all. About 130 years ago, there began a systematic search. At that time, a continuous flow of ancient texts was being found by the native fellahin, and the Egypt Exploration Society, a British non-profit organization, founded in 1882, realized that they needed to send out an expedition team before it was too late. They sent two Oxford scholars, Bernard P. Grenfell, and Arthur S. Hunt, who received permission to search the area south of the farming region in the Faiyūm district. Grenfell chose a site called Behnesa because of its ancient Greek name, Oxyrhynchus. A search of the graveyards and the ruined houses produced nothing. The only place left to search was the town's garbage dumps, which were some 30 feet [9 m] high. It seems to Grenfell and Hunt that all was lost but they decided to try.

Image 3 Grenfell (left) and Hunt (right) in about 1896

In January of 1897, a trial trench (excavation or depression in the ground) was dug, and it only took a few hours before ancient papyrus materials were found. These included letters, contracts, and official documents. The sand had blown over them, covering them, and for nearly 2,000 years, the dry climate had served as a protection for them.

It took only a mere three months to pull out and recover almost two tons of papyri from Oxyrhynchus. They shipped twenty-five large cases back to England. Over the next ten years, these two courageous scholars returned each and every winter, to grow their collection. They discovered ancient classical writing, along with royal ordinances and contracts mixed in with business accounts private letters, shipping lists, as well as fragments of many New Testament manuscripts.

Of what benefit were all these documents? Foremost, the bulk of these documents were written by ordinary people in Koine (common) Greek of the day. Many of the words that would be used in the marketplace, not by the elites appeared in the Greek New Testament Scriptures, which woke scholars up to the fact that Biblical Greek was not some special Greek, but instead, it was the ordinary language of the common people, the man on the street. Thus, by comparing how the words had been used in these papyri, a clearer understanding of Biblical Greek emerged. As of the time of this writing, less than ten percent of these papyri have been published and studied. Most of the papyri were found in the top 10 feet 93 m] of the garbage heap because the other 20 feet [6 m] had been ruined by water from a nearby canal. If we look at it simply, this would mean that the 500 thousand documents found could have been two million in total. Then, we must ponder just how many documents must have come through Oxyrhynchus that were never discarded in the dumps. We have almost a half million papyrus documents (likely there were millions more that did not survive) in garbage dumps in the dry sands of Oxyrhynchus, Egypt.

In the End

The end result is that the New Testament has been preserved in over **5,836** complete or fragmented Greek manuscripts, as well as some **10,000** Latin manuscripts and **9,300 manuscripts** in various other ancient languages, which include Syriac, Slavic, Gothic, Ethiopic, Coptic and Armenian. Some of these are well over 2,000 years old.

CHAPTER 5 How Reliable are the Early Texts of the New Testament?

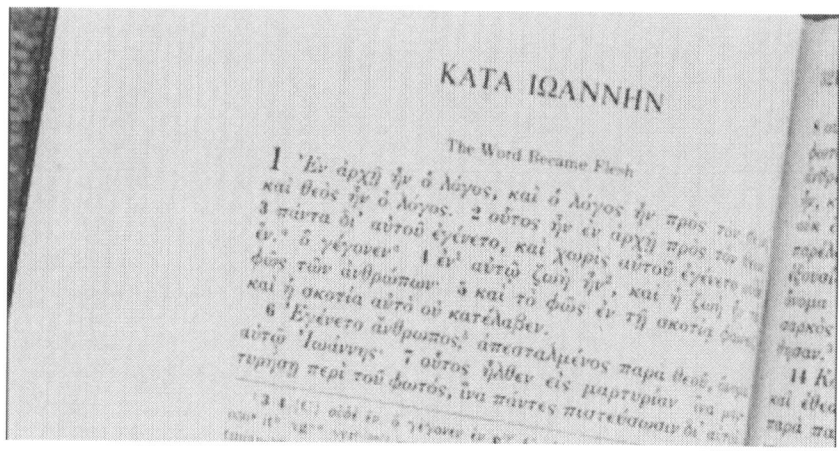

Image 4 The Greek New Testament Gospel of John

Even though many textual scholars credited the Aland's *The Text of the New Testament* with their description of the text as "free," that was not the entire position of the Alands. They did describe different texts' styles, such as "at least normal," "normal," "free," and "strict," seemingly to gauge or weigh the textual faithfulness of each manuscript. However, like Kenyon, they saw a need based on the evidence, which suggested a rethinking of how the evidence should be described,

> We have inherited from the past generation the view that the early text was a 'free' text, and the discovery of the Chester Beatty papyri seemed to confirm this view. When P[45] and P[46] were joined by P[66] sharing the same characteristics, this position seemed to be definitely established. P[75] appeared in contrast to be a loner with its "strict" text anticipating Codex Vaticanus. Meanwhile the other witnesses of the early period had been ignored. It is their collations which have changed the picture so completely.[29]

While we have said this once, it bears repeating, as *some* of the earliest manuscripts that we now have evidence that a professional scribe copied them. *Many* of the other papyri confirm that a semiprofessional hand

---

[29] (Aland and Aland, The Text of the New Testament 1995, 93-5)

copied them, while *most* of these early papyri give evidence of being produced by a copyist who was literate and experienced. Therefore, either literate or semiprofessional copyist did the vast majority of the early extant papyri, with some being done by professionals. As it happened, the few poorly copied manuscripts became known first, establishing a precedent that was difficult for some to shake when the enormous amount of evidence emerged that showed just the opposite.

After a detailed comparison of the papyri, Kurt and Barbara Aland concluded that these manuscripts from the second to the fourth centuries are of three kinds (at least normal, normal, free, and strict). "It is their collations which have changed the picture so completely." (p. 93)

1. **Normal Texts:** The normal text is a relatively faithful tradition (e.g., P[52], which departs from its exemplar only occasionally, as do New Testament manuscripts of every century. It is further represented in P[4], P[5], P[12](?), P[16], P[18], P[20], P[28], P[47], P[72] (1, 2 Peter) and P[87].[30]

2. **Free Texts:** This is a text dealing with the original text in a relatively free manner with no suggestion of a program of standardization (e.g., p[45], p[46] and p[66]), exhibiting the most diverse variants. It is further represented in P[9] (?), P[13](?), P[29], P[37], P[40], P[69], P[72] (Jude) and P[78].[31]

3. **Strict Texts:** These manuscripts transmit the text of the exemplar with meticulous care (e.g., P[75]) and depart from it only rarely. It is further represented in P[1], P[23], P[27], P[35], P[36], P[64+67], P[65](?), and P[70].[32]

Bruce M. Metzger (1914 – 2007) was an editor with Kurt and Barbara Aland of the United Bible Societies' standard Greek New Testament and the Nestle-Aland Greek New Testament. In his *A Textual Commentary on the Greek New Testament*, Second Edition (1971, 1994), and other works, we have his view of the Alexandrian text-type as follows.

The *Alexandrian text*, which Westcott and Hort called the *Neutral text* (a question-begging title), is usually considered to be the best text and the most faithful in preserving the original. Characteristics of the Alexandrian text are brevity and austerity. That is, it is generally shorter than the text of other forms, and it does not exhibit the degree of grammatical and stylistic polishing that is characteristic of the Byzantine type of text. Until recently, the two chief witnesses to the Alexandrian text were codex

---

[30] Ibid., 95

[31] Ibid., 59, 64, 93

[32] Ibid., 64, 95

Vaticanus (B) and codex Sinaiticus (א), parchment manuscripts dating from about the middle of the fourth century. With the acquisition, however, of the Bodmer Papyri, particularly P[66] and P[75], both copied about the end of the second or the beginning of the third century, evidence is now available that the Alexandrian type of text goes back to an archetype that must be dated early in the second century. The Sahidic and Bohairic versions frequently contain typically Alexandrian readings.

It is best if textual scholars focus their attention on the categories the Alands set out, as opposed to their over-generalization that the early period of copying was "uncontrolled" and "free." The Alands' rating system consisted of "at least normal," "normal," "strict," and "free," designed to evaluate the textual faithfulness of each manuscript. It seems that these terms were meant to gauge the level of control that the scribe showed in copying his exemplar. Manuscripts labeled "at least normal" referred to a copyist who at least gave some consideration to his task, namely, producing an accurate copy of the exemplar. "Normal," on the other hand, referred to a copyist who permitted what was deemed a normal number of variants within copying the exemplar. Therefore, "strict" referred to a scribe who allowed very few variants in his copy of the exemplar. Lastly, "free" would refer to a copyist who showed almost no regard for being faithful to the exemplar that he was copying.

It behooves the textual scholar to give much attention to the study of scribal habits, which really began with Ernest Colwell in 1969, who analyzed the scribal habits in P[45], P[66], and P[75] by examining their singular readings.[33] Singular readings are variant readings that are found only in the manuscript being examined, not in any other existing documents. By studying these singular readings of a particular manuscript, we see into the habits of that scribe, namely, his pattern of textual variations, his interactions with the text. Colwell's investigation was followed by a much more extensive study of singular readings by James Royse of the same manuscripts some twelve years later.[34] Then, we had Philip Comfort in his doctoral dissertation in 1997.[35] Comfort explains that his objective was "to

---

[33] Ernest C. Colwell, *"Method in Evaluating Scribal Habits: A Study of P45, P66, P75,"* in *Studies in Methodology in Textual Criticism of the New Testament,* New Testament Tools and Studies 9 (Leiden: Brill, 1969).

[34] James Ronald Royse, *"Scribal Habits in Early Greek New Testament Papyri"* (Ph.D. diss., Graduate Theological Union, 1981). According to Royse, this investigation of singular readings does not apply to lectionaries, patristic sources, and versions, just New Testament papyri, uncials, and minuscules.

[35] Philip Comfort, *"The Scribe as Interpreter: A New Look at New Testament Textual Criticism according to Reader Reception Theory,"* D. Litt. et Phil, dissertation, University of South Africa (1997).

determine what it was in the text that prompted the scribes of P[45], P[66], and P[75] to make individual readings." Comfort suggests that we forgo the categories of the Alands and "that textual critics could use the categories 'reliable,' 'fairly reliable,' and 'unreliable' to describe the textual fidelity of any given manuscript." This author would agree. Moreover, he shows "that many of the early papyri are 'reliable,' several 'fairly reliable,' and a few 'unreliable.'" Comfort then logically explains, "One of the ways of establishing reliability (or lack thereof) is to test a manuscript against one that is generally proven for its textual fidelity. For example, since many scholars have acclaimed the textual fidelity of P[75] (both for intrinsic and extrinsic reasons), it is fair to compare other manuscripts against it in order to determine their textual reliability." (P. Comfort 2005, 268)

How do we know that the critical text NA28 and the UBS5 are reliable? In 1989, Eldon J. Epp noted that the papyri have added virtually no new substantial variants to the variants already known from our later manuscripts.[36] Even with the discovery of many other papyri over the last 25 years, the situation has remained the same. It can be said that after 135 years of early manuscript discoveries since Westcott and Hort of 1881, the above critical editions of the Greek New Testament have gone virtually unchanged. (Hill and Kruger 2012, 5) Hill and Kruger go on to say, "It also means that the fourth-century 'best texts,' the 'Alexandrian' codices Vaticanus and Sinaiticus, have roots extending throughout the entire third century and even into the second." (p. 6)

Reliable Early Texts of the New Testament

The most reliable of the earliest texts are P[1], P[4, 64, 67], P[23], P[27], P[30], P[32], P[35], P[39], P[49, 65], P[70], P[75], P[86], P[87], P[90], P[91], P[100], P[101], P[106], P[108], P[111], P[114], and P[115]. The copyists of these manuscripts allowed very few variants in their copies of the exemplars.[37] They had the ability to make accurate judgments as they went about their copying, resulting in superior texts. Whether their skills in copying were a result of their belief that they were copying a sacred text, or from their training, cannot be known. It could have been a combination of both. These papyri are of great importance when considering textual problems and are considered by many textual scholars to be a good

---

[36] E. J. Epp, 'The Significance of the Papyri for Determining the Nature of the New Testament Text in the Second Century: A Dynamic View of Textual Transmission', in W. L. Petersen, ed., *The Gospel Traditions in the Second Century* (Notre Dame: University of Notre Dame Press, 1989), 101.

[37] In 1988, the Alands, in the second edition of *The Text of the New Testament* (93-95), categorized thirty of the forty-four earliest manuscripts (40 papyri and 4 parchment) as "at least normal," "normal," and "strict," with the other fourteen being categorized as "free" or "like Codex Bezae (D)." At that time, the Alands did not rate P[90] [2nd], P[92], [3rd/4th] and P[95] [3rd], likely because they had only recently been discovered. However, we now have the Aland classification of "strict."

representation of the original wording of the text that was first published by the biblical author. Still, "many of these manuscripts contain singular readings and some 'Alexandrian' polishing, which needs to be sifted out." (P. Comfort 2005, 269) Nevertheless, again, they are the best texts and the most faithful in preserving the original. While it is true that some of the papyri are mere fragments, some contain substantial portions of text. We should note too that text types really did not exist per se in the second century, and it is a mere convention to refer to the papyri as Alexandrian, since the best Alexandrian manuscript, Vaticanus, did exist in the second century by way of P[75].[38] It is not that the Alexandrian text existed, but rather P[75]/Vaticanus evidence that some very strict copying with great care was taking place.[39] Manuscripts that were not of this caliber of strict and careful copying were the result of scribal errors and scribes taking liberties with the text. Therefore, even though P[5] may be categorized as a Western text-type, it is more a matter of negligence in the copying process.

The Aland Classification of Papyri as of 2002[40]

Strict	At Least Normal	Normal	Free	Like D
P1, P23, P27, P35, P39, P64/67, P65(?), P70, P75, P77, P102, P103, P104, P106, P108, P109, P111	P15, P22, P30, P32, P49, P53	P4, P5, P12(?), P16, P18, P20, P28, P47, P52, P72 (1, 2 Pet.), P87, P90, P101, P107	P45, P46, P66, P9(?), P13(?), P29, P37, P40, P69, P72(Jude), P78, P95	P38, P48
Early Uncials 0220	0162, 0189		0171	

---

[38] The Coherence Based Genealogical Method, which was developed by Gerd Mink and assists scholars in developing genealogical trees of manuscripts, will be discussed in far greater detail in Chapter XIII by Wilkins; but we should note here that it has no relation to the traditional text-type model. It is for this reason that scholars such as Holger Strutwolf have suggested that we abandon any references to the manuscripts by the tradition text-types.

[39] "What we do know, from the manuscript evidence, is that several of the earliest Christian scribes were well-trained scribes who applied their training to making reliable texts, both of the Old Testament and the New Testament. We know that they were conscientious to make a reliable text in the process of transcription (as can been seen in manuscripts like P[4+64+67] and P[75]), and we know that others worked to rid the manuscript of textual corruption. This is nowhere better manifested than in P[66], where the scribe himself and the *diorthotes* (official corrector) made over 450 corrections to the text of John. As is explained in the next chapter, the *diorthotes* of P[66] probably consulted other exemplars (one whose text was much like that of P[75]) in making his corrections. This shows a standard Alexandrian scriptoral practice at work in the reproduction of a New Testament manuscript." (P. Comfort, Encountering the Manuscripts: An Introduction to New Testament Paleography and Textual Criticism 2005, 264)

[40] The table is copied from (Hill and Kruger 2012, 11)

As Hill and Kruger put it, "if one accepts the Alands' analyses, in 2002, forty out of fifty-five (or just under 73 percent) of the earliest NT manuscripts had Normal to Strict texts, and fifteen (or just over 27 percent) had Free to Like D texts. The single largest category, consisting of eighteen out of fifty-five (or nearly a third) of the earliest manuscripts, is the category of Strict text." (Hill and Kruger 2012, 11) Therefore, it would be difficult to follow in the footsteps of previous authors who cite the Alands as their source in describing the early period of copying the Greek New Testament as "free," or "wild," "in a state of flux," "chaotic," "a turbid textual morass," and so on.

While the complexities in recovering the original text need to be acknowledged, that is a separate question from whether the concept of an original text is incoherent and should, therefore, be abandoned as a goal of the discipline. Unfortunately, these two questions are often mingled together without distinction. Although recovering the original text faces substantial obstacles (and therefore the results should be qualified), there is little to suggest that it is an illegitimate enterprise. If it were illegitimate, then we would expect the same would be true for Greek and Roman literature outside the New Testament. *The Early Text of the New Testament.* OUP Oxford. Kindle Edition.

It is true that the Jewish copyists, as well as the later Christian copyists, were not led along by the Holy Spirit and therefore their manuscripts were not inerrant, infallible. Errors (textual variants) crept into the manuscripts unintentionally and intentionally. However, the vast majority of the Hebrew Old Testament and Greek New Testament has not been infected with textual errors. For the portions impacted with textual errors, it is the many tens of thousands of copies that we have to help us to weed out the errors. How? Well, not every copyist made the same textual errors. Hence, by comparing the work of different copyists and different manuscripts, textual scholars, we can identify the textual variants (errors), remove those, which leaves us with the original content.

Yes, it would be the greatest discovery of all time if we found the actual original five books that were penned by Moses himself, Genesis through Deuteronomy. However, first, there would be no way of establishing that they were the originals. Second, truth be told, we do not need the originals. We do not need those original documents. What is so important about the documents? Nothing, it is the content on the original documents that we are after. And truly miraculously, we have more copies than needed to do just that. We do not need miraculous preservation because we have miraculous restoration. We now know beyond a reasonable doubt that the Greek New Testament critical text is a 99.5% reflection of the content that was in those ancient original manuscripts.

CHAPTER 6 Was the New Testament Manuscripts Impacted by the Persecution of Early Christianity?

Image 5 Christian Martyrs in the Time of Nero

Jesus had told his followers, "'a slave is not greater than his master.' If they persecuted me, they will also persecute you. If they kept my word, they will keep yours also.'" (John 15:20) Certainly, the growth of Christianity from 120 disciples on Pentecost 33 C.E. to over one million by the middle of the second century was a frightening thought to the pagan mind as well as Judaism. Thus, shortly after the death and resurrection of Jesus Christ, the pagan population, Judaism, and the Roman government began the very persecution of which Jesus had warned. However, it was in the fourth century, under the Roman Emperor Diocletian, that a program of persecution began with the intent of wiping out Christianity. In 303 C.E., Diocletian spread a series of progressively harsh edicts against Christians. This brought about what some historians have called "The Great Persecution."

Diocletian's first edict ordered the burning of copies of the Scriptures and the destruction of Christian houses of worship. Harry Y. Gamble writes, "Diocletian's edict of 303 ordering the confiscation and burning of Christian books is itself important evidence, in both its assumptions and results. At the start of the fourth century, Diocletian took it for granted that every Christian community, wherever it might be, had a collection of books and knew that those books were essential to its viability." (Gamble 1995, 150)

Church historian Eusebius of Caesarea, in his *Ecclesiastical History*, reported, "all things in truth were fulfilled in our day, when we saw with our very eyes the houses of prayer cast down to their foundations from top to bottom, and the inspired and sacred Scriptures committed to the flames in the midst of the market-places." (Cruse 1998, VIII, 1. 9-11.1) The Christians who were most affected by the persecution lived in Palestine, Egypt, and North Africa. In fact, just three months after Diocletian's edict, the mayor of the North African city of Cirta, which was destroyed in the beginning of the 4th century and was rebuilt by the Roman Emperor Constantine the Great, is said to have ordered the Christians to give up all of their "writings of the law" and "copies of scripture." It is quite clear that the intent of Diocletian and local leaders was to wipe out the Word of God.

The authorities had many Christians who obeyed the decrees by handing over their copies of the Scriptures. Nevertheless, some refused to give up their copies of God's Word. Bishop Felix of Thibiuca (d. 303 C.E.) in Africa was martyred during the Great Persecution alongside Audactus, Fortunatus, Januarius, and Septimus.[41] Felix resisted the command of the local magistrate Magnillian (Lat. *Magnillianus*) to surrender his congregation's copies of the Christian Scriptures. One account had Felix and the others being taken to Carthage and decapitated on July 15, 303 C.E. Other Christian leaders deceived the leaders by handing in their pagan writings, safeguarding their Scriptures.

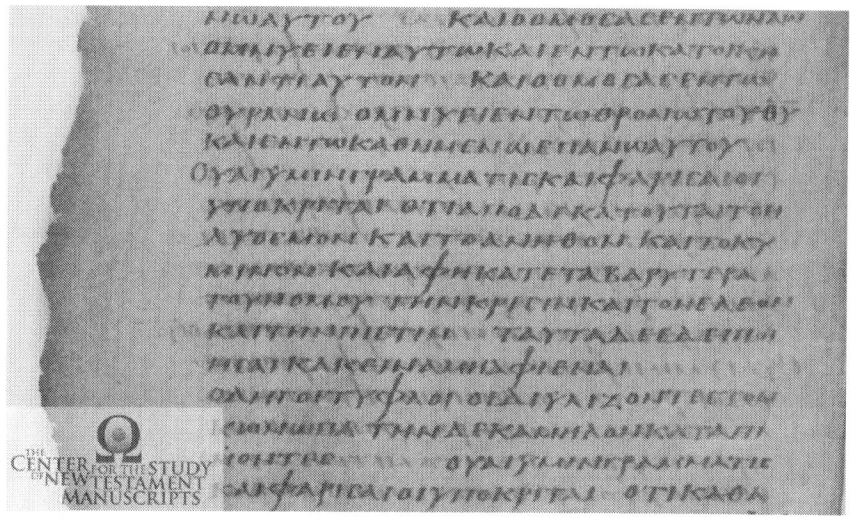

Image 6 The Washington Codex (350-450 C.E.) Matthew 23

---

[41] These men may have been deacons but, apart from their joint martyrdom with Felix, more about their identities are unknown at the time of this writing.

However, when we consider the reading of the Washington Codex of the Gospels manuscript on parchment, it discloses an unusual mixture of text types (Byzantine, Caesarean, Western, and Alexandrian),[42] each represented by large, continuous sections. It was clearly copied from several different manuscripts fragments that had survived the persecution, each possessing a different text type. The Washington Codex might be the result of the sudden persecution of Christians by Emperor Diocletian in the year 303 C.E., wherein the edict to publicly burn all copies of the Scriptures was not fully obeyed by everyone. History tell us that many chose to hide their manuscripts and clearly the survival of so many early manuscripts from the second and third centuries C.E. makes it obvious this was the case. Codex Washingtonus was the work of two scribes only a few decades after Diocletian's persecution (350-450 C.E.),[43] who it would seem copied surviving parts of different manuscripts to produce the text. The first quire of John (John 1:1 to 5:11), a mixture of Alexandrian and Western readings, was lost at some point, which was then rewritten sometime in the seventh century C.E.[44]

The Diocletian persecution was, in the end, unsuccessful. Many Christian libraries escaped the persecution of Diocletian. Two of the best collections today, the Beatty and Bodmer papyri, survived the fires. Alfred Chester Beatty (1875-1968), at the age of 32, had amassed a fortune. As a collector of books, he had over 50 papyrus codices, both religious and secular, which are dated earlier than the fourth century C.E. There are seven consisting of portions of Old Testament books, and three consisting of portions of the New Testament (P^{45} c. 250, P^{46} c. 175–225, and P^{47} c. 250-300). Martin Bodmer (1899-1971) was also a wealthy collector, who discovered twenty-two papyri in Egypt in 1952 which contained parts of the Old and New Testaments, as well as other early Christian literature. Particularly noteworthy are the New Testament Bodmer papyri, which consist of P^{66} dating to c. 200 C.E. and P^{75} dating to c. 175 C.E. Many in rural Egypt would have heard of the persecution in Alexandria, likely making great efforts to remove their manuscripts from their congregations, hiding them until the persecution was lifted.

---

[42] Matthew. 1–28; Luke 8:13–24:53 – Byzantine text-type; Mark 1:1–5:30 – Western text-type similar to old-Latin Versions; Mark 5:31 – 16:20 – Caesarean text-type near to P45; Luke 1:1 – 8:12, and John 5:12–21:25 – Alexandrian text-type; John 1:1–5:11 – mixed with some Alexandrian and Western readings.

[43] Kurt Alan; Barbara Aland (1995). *The Text of the New Testament: An Introduction to the Critical Editions and to the Theory and Practice of Modern Textual Criticism.* Erroll F. Rhodes (trans.). Grand Rapids: William B. Eerdmans Publishing Company. p. 113.

[44] Bruce M. Metzger; Bart D. Ehrman (2005). *The Text of the New Testament: Its Transmission, Corruption and Restoration* (4 ed.). New York – Oxford: Oxford University Press. p. 80.

The men who were known as the *readers* in the early Christian congregations, who read from the Scriptures during the meeting, carried the burden of preserving the Word of God beyond preserving accurate copies.[45] They also would have guarded them during times of persecution. Because of the mass persecution against Alexandria, Egypt,[46] we owe the primary preservation of our New Testament manuscripts to those congregations within rural Egypt. During times of persecution, manuscripts would not have been housed in the facilities of the congregation but rather would have been hidden in homes. Because of the dry sands of Egypt, the professional scribal practices, and the courage of the Christians, we not only owe the Egyptian Christians for the preservation of the New Testament but also for the original *words* that made up the New Testament. If we look at the manuscripts copied right after the Diocletian persecution (Codex Vaticanus and Sinaitic c. 350 C.E.), they are reflective of the manuscripts from rural Egypt that survived, such as P4, 64, 67 from Coptos, P13 from Oxyrhynchus, and P46 from Fayum, and P75 from Abu Mana. (P. W. Comfort 1992, 16-17)

What we do know is that by the time we get to the era of the Diocletian persecution (February 23, 303 – July 25, 306.), the authorities were well aware that there were still many copies of the New Testament throughout the Roman Empire. Otherwise, there would have been no need on February 24, 303 for Diocletian's first "Edict against the Christians" to be published. Diocletian thought he could eradicate Christianity by destroying its sacred writings. After the persecution of Diocletian and Constantine succeeding his father on July 25, 306, Constantine immediately ended any persecutions that were ongoing at that time and offered Christians complete restitution of what they had lost under the persecution. When Constantine issued the Edict of Milan of 313 C.E., Christianity was legalized in the Roman Empire, at which point, the church would have seen the need to dramatically increase the number of copies of the Scriptures. Now that Christianity was no longer being persecuted, Christian scribes could openly make copies of the New Testament manuscripts.

In 331 C.E., Constantine had ordered Eusebius to prepare fifty copies of entire Bible to be written on prepared parchment for distribution to the churches he intended to build in Constantinople. (Eus., Vit. Const. 4.36.2) From this small order placed by Constantine, we can only imagine how

---

[45] Some may have been scribes as well but not all. Retaining accurate, fresh copies for the congregation entailed reaching out to scribes or scriptoriums, to acquire copies for their congregation.

[46] This is not to say that no manuscripts survived the persecution in Alexandria; it is possible that some came through the flames.

many copies had been made in the churches throughout the entire Roman Empire. It has been estimated that there were some fifteen hundred to two thousand manuscripts of the Greek New Testament copied in the fourth century C.E. (J. Duplacy) While we certainly took a loss in the number of copies that may have come down to us today as a result of ongoing sporadic persecution of Christianity in those first two and a half centuries after the death of the apostle Paul at the hands of the Roman Emperor Nero in about 65 C.E. up unto Diocletian (303-306 C.E.), there is little doubt that the storehouse of Greek original language manuscripts (5,836) that we do possess are an envy of the secular historians, who have next to nothing in comparison.

CHAPTER 7 How Did the Spread of Early Christianity Impact the Text of the New Testament

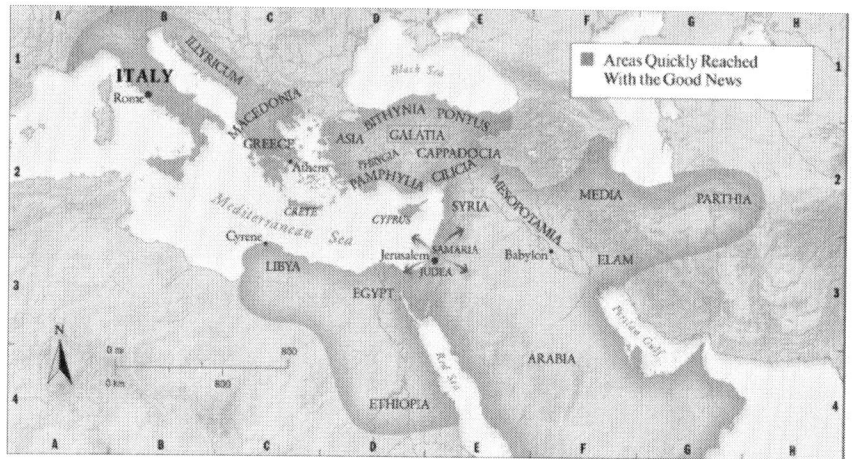

Image 7 The Spread of Christianity by the Second-Century C.E.

The Apostasy

Within just a few short decades after the death of the apostle John, divisions were already evident among the early Christians. Historian Will and Ariel Durant write: "Celsus [Greek Philosopher and second-century opponent of Christianity] himself had sarcastically observed that Christians were 'split up into ever so many factions, each individual desiring to have his own party.' About 187 AD Irenaeus listed twenty varieties of Christianity; about 384 AD Epiphanius counted eighty." (*The Story of Civilization: Part III, Caesar and Christ*) While this and what lies below is all true, the first century Christianity that Jesus Christ started, and the apostles grew went from 120 Christians in the upper room of Pentecost 33 C.E.[47] to shortly over one million by 130 C.E. This in a world of only a one hundred million in population.

---

[47] B.C.E. means "before the Common Era," which is more accurate than B.C. ("before Christ"). C.E. denotes "Common Era," often called A.D., for anno Domini, meaning "in the year of our Lord."

2 Thessalonians 2:1a, 3 Updated American Standard Version (UASV)

2 Now we request you, brothers, with regard to the coming of our Lord Jesus Christ ... **3** Let no one deceive you in any way, for it will not come unless the apostasy comes first, and the man of lawlessness is revealed, the son of destruction,

Apostasy: (Gr. *apostasia*) The term literally means "to stand away from" and is used to refer to ones who 'stand away from the truth.' It is abandonment, a rebellion, an apostasy, a refusal to accept or acknowledge true worship. In Scripture, this is used primarily concerning the one who rises up in defiance of the only true God and his people, working in opposition to the truth. – Ac 21:21; 2 Thess. 2:3.

On this text, New Testament scholar Knute Larson writes, "Before that great day comes, Paul declared, the rebellion must occur. The word used here is *apostasia* or apostasy. Before the day of the Lord, there will be a great denial, a deliberate turning away by those who profess to belong to Christ. It will be a rebellion. Having once allied themselves with Christ, they will abandon him. Within the recognized church there will come a time when people will forsake their faith. Throughout history, there have been defections from the faith. But the apostasy about which he wrote to the Thessalonians would be of greater magnitude and would signal the coming of the end." (Larson 2000, 105)

The apostle Paul says to the Ephesian elders; there is but "one Lord, one faith, one baptism." (Eph. 4:5) Paul penned those words about 60 C.E., and he was informing them that there was but one Christian faith. Yet, today we see more varieties of Christian faith than we care to count, all claiming that they are the truth and the way. Whenever a brave soul dares to be truthful and bring up that there are doctrinal differences, different doctrinal position, and different standards of conduct, he is shouted down as an alarmist. They claim that most of these denominations are the same on the essential doctrines, i.e., the salvation doctrines. Well, this actually is not true and is an attempt at hiding the truth, because even the salvation doctrines have anywhere from three to five different interpretations. Regardless, we must concern ourselves with a crucial question from Jesus Christ, "when the Son of Man comes, will he find faith on earth?" (Lu 18:8) This is a whole other discussion. We concern ourselves with how these divisions came about in the first place.

As has already been stated in another blog article, but bears repeating, the blame lies with Satan. He attempted to have Jesus killed as a baby, he tempted Jesus in the wilderness after his baptism, and he attempted persecution right from the start. Peter wrote, "Be sober-minded; be watchful. Your adversary, the devil, prowls around like a roaring lion, seeking someone to devour." (1 Pet. 5:8) Initially, the persecution of this young Christian body came from Jewish religious leaders, and then from the Roman Empire itself. With "all authority in heaven" (Matt. 28:20) Jesus watched on, as the Holy Spirit guided and directed them, this infancy Christian congregation endured the best that Satan and his henchman had to offer. (See Rev. 1:9; 2:3, 19) As we know from Scripture, Satan is not one to give up, so he devised a new plan, divide and conquer. Yes, he would cause divisions within the Christian congregation. Satan broke out the ultimate weapon— the apostasy. We need not to believe that all of a sudden, the apostasy came into the Christian congregation. No, Jesus was watching from heaven, and he made sure that he warned them while he was here on earth of what was to come, and he made the young Christian congregation aware of what was coming and when it was getting started.— Colossians 1:18

In the Greek New Testament, the noun "apostasy" (Gr., *apostasia*) has the sense of "desertion, abandonment or rebellion." (Acts 21:21) There it predominantly is alluding to abandonment; a drawing away from or abandoning of pure worship.

"[Jesus] Be Aware of False Prophets . . .

[Peter] There Will Be False Teachers Among You."

Matthew 7:15 Updated American Standard Version (UASV)

¹⁵ "Beware of the false prophets, who come to you in sheep's clothing, but inwardly are ravenous wolves.

Jesus was well aware of what Satan would try to accomplish step-by-step, and that divisions through those from within were on the list. New Testament scholar Stuart K. Weber says, "Jesus had an important reason for inserting the wolf metaphor (Acts 20:27–31)—to alert his listeners to the danger of a false prophet. If the false prophets were thought of as a source of bad fruit, then the disciples might think it was enough simply to recognize and ignore the false prophet, refusing to consume his bad fruit, and awaiting God's judgment on him. But the wolf metaphor attributes a more active and malicious motive to the false prophet. He is actually an enemy of the sheep, and, if not confronted, will get his way by destroying the sheep." (Weber 2000, 101)

Weber mentions Acts 20:28-30, where Paul, about **56 C.E.**, warned the Ephesian elders,

Acts 20:28-30 Updated American Standard Version (UASV)

²⁸ Pay careful attention to yourselves and to all the flock, in which the Holy Spirit has made you overseers, to care for the congregation[6] of

God, which he obtained with the blood of his own Son.[48] 29 I know that after my departure fierce wolves will come in among you, not sparing the flock; 30 and **from among your own selves** men will arise, **speaking twisted things**, to **draw away the disciples after them.**

Yes, these, who standoff from the Truth and the Way, would not be seeking their own disciples, but rather they would be seeking, "to draw away the disciples after them." i.e., the disciples of Christ. Jesus was well aware that the easiest way to defeat any group is to divide them, and so was Satan, who had been watching humanity for over 4,000 years, and especially the Israelites (Isaac and Ishmael / Jacob and Esau / Israel and Judah), as "Satan disguises himself as an angel of light. So, it is no surprise if his servants, also, disguise themselves as servants of righteousness." – 2 Corinthians 11:14-15.

The apostle Peter also spoke of these things about **64 C.E.**, "there will be false teachers among you, who will secretly bring in destructive heresies ... in their greed they will exploit you with false words." (2 Pet. 2:1, 3) These abandoned the faithful words, became false teachers, rising within the Christian congregation, sharing their corrupting influence, intending to hide, disguise, or mislead.

These dire warnings by Jesus and the New Testament Authors had their beginnings in the first century C.E. Yes, they began small, but burst forth on the scene in the second century.

Gnostic Beliefs

Marcion (85-c.160) was a semi-Gnostic, who believed that the teachings of Jesus were irreconcilable with the actions of the God of the Old Testament. He viewed the God of the Old Testament, Jehovah, to be vicious, violent and cruel, an oppressor who gave out material rewards to those worshiping him. In contrast, Marcion described the New Testament God, Jesus Christ, as a perfect God, the God of unadulterated love and compassion, of kindness and quick to forgive.

Montanus (late second century) was a "prophet" from Asia Minor, who believed that their revelation came directly from the Holy Spirit, which superseded the authority of Jesus, Paul, Peter, John, James, anyone really. They believed in the imminent return of Christ and the setting up of the New Jerusalem in Pepuza. He was more concerned about Christian conduct than he was Christian doctrine, wanting to get back to the Christian values of the first century. However, he took this to the extreme, just as John Calvin would some 1,300 years later in the 16th century. Montanism was a

---

[48] Lit *with the blood of his Own.*

movement focused on prophecy, especially the founder's views, being seen as the light for their time. They believed that the apostle and prophets had the power to forgive sin.

Valentinus (c.100-c.160) was a Greek poet, who founded his school in Rome, and most prominent early Christian gnostic theologian. He claimed that though Jesus' heavenly (spiritual) body was of Mary, he was not actually born from her. This belief came about because Gnostics viewed all matter as evil. Therefore, if Jesus had really been a real human person with a physical body, he would have been evil. Another form of Gnosticism was Docetism, which claimed that Jesus Christ was not a real person, i.e., it was a mere appearance and illusion, which would have included his death and resurrection.

Manes (c. 216-274) was the prophet and the founder of Manichaeism, a gnostic religion. He sought to combine elements of Christianity, Buddhism, and Zoroastrianism, based on a rigid dualism of good and evil, locked in an eternal struggle. He believed that salvation is possible through education, self-denial, fasting, and chastity. He also believed that he was an "apostle of Jesus Christ," (Ramsey 2006, 272) although, strictly speaking, his religion was not a movement of Christian Gnosticism in the earlier approach.

Beginning with the Council of Nicaea in 325 C.E., Emperor Constantine legalized Christianity in an attempt at reunited the empire. He fully understood that religious division was a threat to the continuation of the Roman Empire. However, it was Emperor Theodosius I (347 – 395 C.E.), who banned paganism and imposed Christianity as the State religion of the Roman Empire. The Roman Catholic Church can trace its existence back to the council of Nicaea in 325 C.E. at best. Protestantism had its beginnings in the Reformation of the 16th century. However, there were dissensions in within Catholicism for a thousand years.

Returning to the First Century

The early Christian congregations were not isolated from one another. The Roman roads and maritime travel connected all the regions from Rome to Greece, to Asia, to Syria and Palestine, and Egypt.[49] Following the days of Pentecost 33 C.E., Jewish or Jewish proselyte Christians returned to Egypt with the good news of Christ (Acts 2:10). Three years after that, the Ethiopian eunuch traveled home with the good news as well (Acts 8:26–

---

[49] People of the first three centuries sent and received letters and books from all over the Roman Empire. Hurtado has given us two examples: the Shepherd of Hermas was written in Rome and found its way to Egypt within a few decades; Irenaeus' Against Heresies was written in Gaul and made it to Egypt (Oxyrhynchus) within short order.

39). Apollos of Alexandria, Egypt, a renowned speaker, left Egypt with the knowledge of John the Baptizer and arrived in Ephesus in about 52 C. E. (Acts 18:24-25) The apostle Paul traveled approximately 10,282 miles throughout the Roman Empire establishing congregations.[50] The apostles were a restraint to the apostasy and division within the whole of the first-century Christian congregation (2 Thess. 2:6-7; 1 John 2:18). It was not until the second century that the next generation of Christian leaders gradually caused divisions.[51] However, the one true Christianity that Jesus started and the apostles established was strong, active, and able to defend against Gnosticism, Roman persecution, and Jewish opposition.

It is conceivable that by 55 C.E. there would have been a thriving congregation in Alexandrian Egypt, with its huge Jewish population.[52] "Now those who had been scattered because of the persecution that arose over Stephen went through as far as Phoenicia and Cyprus and Antioch, speaking the word to no one except Jews" (Acts 11:19). While this indicates a traveling north to Antioch, it does not negate traveling south to Egypt. Antioch obviously is mentioned because it played a significant role as a commencement for first-century Christianity, in particular for the apostle Paul.

The Coptic Church claims the Gospel writer Mark as its founder and first patriarch. Tradition has it that he preached in Egypt just before the middle of the first century. At any rate, Christianity spread to Egypt and North Africa at an early date. In fact, it became a prominent religious center, with a noted scholar named Pantaenus, who founded a catechetical school in Alexandria, Egypt, about 160 C.E. In about 180 C.E. another prominent scholar, Clement of Alexandria, took over his position. Clement put this religious, educational institution on the map as a possible center for the whole of the Christian church throughout the Roman Empire. The persecution that came circa the year 202 C.E. forced Clement to flee Alexandria, but one of the most noted scholars of early Christian history, Origen, replaced him. In addition, Origen took this scholarly environment to Caesarea in 231 C.E. and started yet another prominent school and scriptorium (i.e., a room for copying manuscripts).

---

[50] http://orbis.stanford.edu/

[51] This apostasy and divisiveness did not just come into the Christian congregation from nowhere. It started developing in the first century but was restrained by apostolic authority.

[52] Macquarie University, *Ancient History Documentary Research Center* (AHDRC), Papyri from the Rise of Christianity in Egypt (PCE),

http://www.anchist.mq.edu.au/doccentre/PCEhomepage.html.

What does all this mean? While we cannot know absolutely, textual scholar Philip W. Comfort[53] and others believe that the very early Alexandrian manuscripts that we now possess are a reflection of what would have been found throughout the whole of the Greco-Roman Empire about 125–300 C.E. If we were to discover other early manuscripts from Antioch, Constantinople, Carthage, or Rome, they would be very similar to the early Alexandrian manuscripts. This means that these early manuscripts are a primary means of establishing the original text, and we are in a far better position today than were Westcott and Hort in 1881.

In addition, we can assume an effort on the part of copyists to preserve the originals unchanged, because the authors themselves spoke of their writings as being authoritative and said that no one should alter what they had published or taught. The apostle Paul wrote to the Galatians that they should consider as "accursed" anyone (even angels) who proclaimed a gospel contrary to the one they had preached. (Gal. 1:6-9) Paul went on to write, "the gospel that was preached by me is not according to man [I.e., human origin]. For I neither received it from man, nor was I taught it, but I received it through a revelation [Lit., uncovering; disclosure] of Jesus Christ." (Gal. 1:11-12) The apostle Paul charged that 'the Corinthian Christians had put up with false teachers, readily enough, who proclaim another Jesus and another gospel.' (2 Cor. 11:3-4) Paul and Silas wrote to the Thessalonians that they constantly thanked God that when the Thessalonians received the word of God, which they had heard from them, they accepted it not as the word of men, but for what it really was, the **word of God**. (1Thess. 2:3) Paul then closed that letter by commanding them "by the Lord, have this letter read aloud to all the brothers." (1 Thess. 5:27) In 2 Thessalonians Paul 'requested that they not be quickly shaken from their composure or be disturbed either by a spirit or a word or a letter as if from us.' (2:2) Paul closed the letter with a greeting in his own hand, to authenticate it. (3:17) Lastly, John closed the book of Revelation with a warning to everyone about adding to or taking away from what he had written therein. (Rev. 22:18-19) The New Testament authors were well aware that future scribes could intentionally alter the Word of God, so they warned them of the consequences.

Let's look at yet another author of the New Testament. The apostle Peter wrote about **64 C.E.**,

2 Peter 1:12-18 Updated American Standard Version (UASV)

[12] Therefore, I will always be ready to remind you of these things, though you know them and are established in the truth that is present with

---

[53] Philip W. Comfort, *The Quest for the Original Text of the New Testament* (Eugene, Oregon: Wipf and Stock Publishers, 1992).

71

you. [13] I consider it right, as long as I am in this tabernacle,[54] to stir you up by way of reminder, [14] knowing that the putting off of my tabernacle[55] is soon,[56] just as also our Lord Jesus Christ made clear to me. [15] So I will make every effort so that after my departure, you may be able to recall these things for yourselves.[57]

Prophetic Word Made More Sure

[16] For we did not follow cleverly devised myths when we made known to you the power and coming[58] of our Lord Jesus Christ, but we were eyewitnesses of his majesty. [17] For when he received honor and glory from God the Father, and the voice was brought[59] to him by the Majestic Glory, "This is my beloved Son, with whom I am well pleased," [18] and we ourselves heard this very voice brought from heaven, when we were with him on the holy mountain.

Peter was making it clear that he was sharing firsthand accounts and not devised tales. Here again, like the other New Testament authors, Peter warned his readers of false teachers, who corrupted the truth and distorted the Scriptures, such as Paul's letters. Like Paul and John, Peter warned that this would be done to the offenders' own destruction.

2 Peter 3:15-16 Updated American Standard Version (UASV)

[15] and regard the patience of our Lord as salvation; just as also our beloved brother Paul, according to the wisdom given him, wrote to you, [16] as also in all his letters, speaking in them of these things, in which are some things hard to understand, which the untaught and unstable distort, as they do also the rest of the Scriptures, to their own destruction.

Yes, "It is especially interesting that Peter writes of the distortion of Paul's letters along with 'the other Scriptures.' The implication is that the

---

[54] Or *earthly dwelling* or *tent*; that is, *his earthly body*

[55] Or *earthly dwelling* or *tent*; that is, *his earthly body*

[56] Or *is coming swiftly*

[57] Lit *to call these things to remembrance*

[58] **Presence; Coming:** (Gr. *parousia*) The Greek word literally means," which is derived from *para*, meaning "with," and *ousia*, meaning "being." It denotes both an "arrival" and a consequent "presence with." Depending on the context, it can mean "presence," "arrival," "appearance," or "coming." In some contexts this word is describing the presence of Jesus Christ in the last days, i.e., from his ascension in 33 C.E. up unto his second coming, with the emphasis being on his second coming, the end of the age of Satan's reign of terror over the earth. We do not know the day nor the hours of this second coming. (Matt 24:36) It covers a marked period of time with the focus on the end of that period.–Matt. 24:3, 27, 37, 39; 1 Cor. 15:23; 16:17; 2 Cor. 7:6-7; 10:10; Php 1:26; 2:12; 1 Thess. 2:19; 3:13; 4:15; 5:2.

[59] Or *borne* or *made*

letters of Paul were already regarded as Scripture at the time Peter wrote."[60] Verse 16 shows that Peter

...is aware of several Pauline letters. This knowledge again raises the dating issue. We know that Paul himself on one occasion had requested that churches share his letters: 'After this letter has been read to you, see that it is also read in the church of the Laodiceans and that you, in turn, read the letter from Laodicea' (Col 4:16). However, it is a big jump in time from Colossians to the first concrete evidence we have of people who know more than one letter. This evidence shows up in *1 Clement*, who not only knows Romans but can also write to the Corinthians, 'Take up the epistle of the blessed Apostle Paul' (*1 Clem.*[61] 47:1). It appears later in *2 Clement* and in Ignatius's *Ephesians*.[62] Thus, we are on solid ground when we accept that a collection of the Pauline letters existed by the end of the first century.[63] It is also likely that some Pauline letters circulated independently of a collection (which is what one would expect as one church hears that another has a letter that might prove helpful in their situation),[64] and that there were collections of a few Pauline letters before there was a collection of all of his letters.[65] All of this is quite logical since Paul was a valued teacher in his circle of communities and, as he left an area and especially as he died, his letters were his continuing voice. Thus churches would share letters and, as they obtained funds (a few hundred dollars to a couple thousand dollars in today's money), they would make copies. Copies would turn into collections, especially since it was possible to use one scroll for several of the shorter letters. Probably by the end of the first

---

[60] Allen Black and Mark C. Black, *1 & 2 Peter*, The College Press NIV Commentary (Joplin, MO: College Press Pub., 1998), 2 Pe 3:16.

[61] *1 Clem.* First Epistle of Clement to the Corinthians

[62] Ignatius, *Eph.* 12:2, refers to Paul, "who in all his Epistles makes mention of you in Christ Jesus." (Although one wonders how Ignatius thought the Ephesians were mentioned in every Pauline letter he knew.) On the evidence for 2 Clement's knowledge of a collection, see Karl P. Donfried, *The Setting of Second Clement in Early Christianity* (NovTSup 38; Leiden: E. J. Brill, 1974), 93–95.

[63] Jack Finegan, "The Original Form of the Pauline Collection," *HTR* 49 (1956) 85–104. See also Walter Schmithals, "Zur Abfassung und ältesten Sammlung der pauli nischen Hauptbriefe" ["On the Composition and Earliest Collection of the Major Epistles of Paul"], *ZNW* 51 (1960) 225–45.

[64] Harry Gamble, "The Redaction of the Pauline Letters and the Formation of the Pauline Corpus," *JBL* 94 (1971) 403–18.

[65] Mary Lucetta Mowry, "The Early Circulation of Paul's Letters," *JBL* 63 (1944) 73–86.

century, the complete collection (i.e., all extant letters) was circulating to at least a limited degree (remember, these copies did not come cheap). The issue is which stage in this process 2 Peter is indicating.[66]

This author would argue that the stage Peter to which was referring was the time when "there were collections of a few Pauline letters before there was a collection of all of his letters." It is most likely that Peter's first letter was written about **62-64 C.E.**, while **Peter's second letter was written about 64 C.E.**[67] At the time Peter penned his second letter, several of Paul's letters from the 50s was available to Peter (Romans [56], 1 & 2 Corinthians [55], Galatians [50-52], and 1 & 2 Thessalonians [50, 51]). He could have had access to those from the early 60s as well (Ephesians [60-61], Philippians [60-61], Colossians [60-61], Titus [61-64], Philemon [60-61], and Hebrews [61]). The only ones that were clearly unavailable would have been 1 & 2 Timothy [61, 64] and possibly Titus [61-64]. Thus, from Peter's reference to "in all his [Paul's] letters, speaking in them of these things," we garner several insights. It highly suggests (1) there were collections of Paul's letters, (2) Peter and the early church viewed them as "Scripture" in the same sense as the Old Testament Scriptures, (3) they were not to be changed, and (4) that apostolic authors' written works were being collected and preserved for posterity.

Second-Century Manuscripts: Once we enter the second century almost all firsthand witnesses of Jesus Christ would have died, and most of the younger traveling companions, fellow workers and students of the apostles, would be advancing into old age. However, there were some, like Polycarp who was born to Christian parents about 69 C.E. in Asia Minor, in Smyrna. As he grew into a man, he became known for his kindness, self-discipline, compassionate treatment of others, and thorough study of God's Word. Soon enough he became an elder in the Christian congregation at Smyrna. Polycarp was very fortunate to live in a time when he was able to learn from the apostles themselves. In fact, the apostle John was one of his teachers.

By any standard, Polycarp must be reckoned as one of the more notable figures in the early postapostolic church. Already bishop of Smyrna in Asia Minor when his friend and mentor, Ignatius of Antioch [c. 35 C.E. – c. 108 C.E.], addressed one of his letters to him (ca. A.D. 110; cf. above, p. 131), he died a martyr's

---

[66] Peter H. Davids, *The Letters of 2 Peter and Jude*, The Pillar New Testament Commentary (Grand Rapids, MI: William B. Eerdmans Pub. Co., 2006), 302–303.

[67] Clinton E. Arnold, *Zondervan Illustrated Bible Backgrounds Commentary: Hebrews to Revelation.*, vol. 4 (Grand Rapids, MI: Zondervan, 2002), 153.

death (see the *Martyrdom of Polycarp*) several decades later at age eighty-six (ca. 155–160), having served as bishop for at least forty and possibly sixty or more years. Irenaeus (who met Polycarp as a child) and Eusebius both considered him a significant link in the chain of orthodox apostolic tradition. His life and ministry spanned the time between the end of the apostolic era and the emergence of catholic [i.e., universal] Christianity, and he was deeply involved in the central issues and challenges of this critical era: the growing threat of persecution by the state, the emerging Gnostic movement (he is particularly known for his opposition to one of the movement's most charismatic and theologically innovative teachers, Marcion), the development of the monepiscopal form of ecclesiastical organization, and the formation of the canon of the New Testament. Polycarp's only surviving document[68] is a letter to the Philippians, written in response to a letter from them (cf. 3.1; 13.1). It reveals, in addition to a direct and unpretentious style and a sensitive pastoral manner, a deep indebtedness to the Scriptures (in the form of the Septuagint) and early Christian writings, including *1 Clement* (with which Polycarp seems to be particularly familiar).[69] While apparently no New Testament books are cited as 'Scripture' (the reference to Ephesians in 12.1 is a possible exception), the manner in which Polycarp refers to them indicates that he viewed them as authoritative documents.[70]

Christ "gave gifts to men." "He gave some as apostles, and some as prophets, and some as evangelists, and some as pastors and teachers" (Eph. 4:8, 11-13, NASB). The Father moved these inspired ones along by Holy Spirit, as they set forth God's Word for the Christian congregation, "to stir [them] up by way of reminder," repeating many things already written in the Scriptures (2 Pet. 1:12-13; 3:1; Rom 15:15). Thus, we have internal New Testament evidence from Second Peter circa **64 C.E.** that "there were collections of a few Pauline letters before there was a collection of all of his letters." Outside of Scripture, we find evidence of a collection of at least

---

[68] The attempt by H. von Campenhausen ("Polykarp und die Pastoralen," repr. *Aus der Frühzeit des Christentums* [Tübingen: Mohr/Siebeck, 1963], 197–252) to show that Polycarp also authored the pastoral Epistles has met with little acceptance.

[69] Schoedel (*Polycarp*, 4–5) suggests that it is "fairly certain" that the letter "reflects more or less direct contact" with the following writings: Psalms, Proverbs, Isaiah, Jeremiah, Ezekiel, Tobit, Matthew, Luke, Acts, Romans, 1–2 Corinthians, Galatians, Ephesians, Philippians, 1–2 Timothy, 1 John, 1 Peter, and *1 Clement*. Metzger (*Canon*, 61–62) adds to the New Testament list 2 Thessalonians and Hebrews while deleting Acts and 2 Corinthians.

[70] Michael William Holmes, *The Apostolic Fathers: Greek Texts and English Translations*, Third ed. (Grand Rapids, MI: Baker Books, 2007), 272–273.

ten Pauline letters that were collected together by **90-100 C.E.**[71] We can be certain that the early Christians were collecting the inspired Christian Scriptures as early as the middle of the first century C.E. to the early second century C.E.

Clement of Rome (c. 96 C.E.) was acquainted with Paul's letter to the church at Corinth and said that Paul wrote under the inspiration of the Spirit. Thus, we have Clement of Rome (c. 30-100 C.E.), Polycarp of Smyrna (69-155 C.E.), and Ignatius of Antioch (c. 35 C.E. – c. 108 C.E.), who wove Scripture of the Greek New Testament into their writings, showing their view of them as inspired Scripture. Justin Martyr, who died about 165 C.E., used the expression "it is written" when quoting from Matthew. Theophilus of Antioch, who died about 181 C.E., declared "concerning the righteousness which the law enjoined, confirmatory utterances are found both with the prophets and in the Gospels because they all spoke inspired by one Spirit of God."[72] Theophilus then used such expressions as "**says the Gospel**" (quoting Matt, 5:28, 32, 44, 46; 6:3) and "**the divine word** gives us instructions, in order that "we may lead a quiet and peaceable life."[73] And it teaches us to render all things to all,[74] "honour to whom honour, fear to whom fear, tribute to whom tribute; to owe no man anything, but to love all."[75]

Once we reach the middle to the end of the second century C.E., it comes down to whether those who came before **would stress the written documents as Scripture by**

- the apostles, who had been personally selected by Jesus (Matthew, John, and Peter),

- Paul, who was later selected as an apostle by the risen Jesus himself,

- the half-brothers of Jesus Christ (James and Jude),

---

[71] Jack Finegan, "The Original Form of the Pauline Collection," *HTR* 49 (1956) 85–104. See also Walter Schmithals, "Zur Abfassung und ältesten Sammlung der pauli nischen Hauptbriefe" ["On the Composition and Earliest Collection of the Major Epistles of Paul"], *ZNW* 51 (1960) 225–45.

[72] Theophilus of Antioch, "Theophilus to Autolycus," in *Fathers of the Second Century: Hermas, Tatian, Athenagoras, Theophilus, and Clement of Alexandria (Entire)*, ed. Alexander Roberts, James Donaldson, and A. Cleveland Coxe, trans. Marcus Dods, vol. 2, The Ante-Nicene Fathers (Buffalo, NY: Christian Literature Company, 1885), 114.

[73] 1 Tim. 2:2

[74] Rom. 13:7, 8

[75] Theophilus of Antioch, "Theophilus to Autolycus," in *Fathers of the Second Century: Hermas, Tatian, Athenagoras, Theophilus, and Clement of Alexandria (Entire)*, ed. Alexander Roberts, James Donaldson, and A. Cleveland Coxe, trans. Marcus Dods, vol. 2, The Ante-Nicene Fathers (Buffalo, NY: Christian Literature Company, 1885), 115.

- as well as Mark and Luke, who were close associates and traveling companions of Paul and Peter.

We can see from the above that this largely was the case. We know that major church leaders across the Roman Empire had done just that. We know, for example, that Irenaeus of Asia Minor (180 C.E.) fully accepted 25 of 27 books of the New Testament but had some doubt about Hebrews and uncertainty about James. We know that Clement of Alexandria (190 C.E.) fully accepted 26 of 27 books of the New Testament but may not have been aware of 3 John. We know that Tertullian of North Africa (207 C.E.) fully accepted 24 of 27 books but may not have been aware of 2 and 3 John, or Jude. We know that Origen of Alexandria (230 C.E.) and Eusebius of Palestine (320 C.E.) fully accepted all 27 books of the New Testament. It has been estimated that by the close of the second century C.E., there were over 60,000 copies of major parts of the Greek New Testament in existence. This is an enormous number, even if it was only one in every fifty professing Christians who possessed a copy.

However, would there be evidence that these church leaders, going back to the days of the apostles, would influence the copyists? Moreover, were the copyists professionals? (more on this in a moment) In other words, even if some of the copyists did not see the documents as Scripture, would the church leaders, and long-standing traditions, motivate them to copy the documents with accuracy? In addition, would the professional scribe copy accurately even if he did not view them as Scripture? And if the scribe did view the texts as Scripture, the inspired Word of God, was it plenary inspiration (every word), or that the meaning was inspired? Generally speaking, from what we know about the Alexandrian scribes, they would have sought to reproduce an accurate copy regardless of their views. We can say that there were other scribes, who saw the message as inspired; thus, their focus was not on retaining every single word, nor word order. It seems that they felt they could alter the words without damaging the intended meaning of the author. These copyists added and removed words here and there, rearranged words, and substituted words, presumably in the hope of improving the text but not intending to alter the meaning. It also has to be acknowledged that there were some untrained copyists who simply produced inaccurate copies, regardless of how they viewed the text.

Then, there were scribes who willfully altered the text, with the intention of improving it. Some were seeking to harmonize the gospel accounts. An extreme example would be Tatian, a noteworthy, apologetic writer of the second century C.E. In an account of his conversion to nominal Christianity, Tatian states, "I sought how I might be able to discover the truth," which points to his intent. About 170 C.E., Tatian compiled a harmonized account of the life and ministry of Jesus Christ, combining the four Gospels into a single narrative (Diatessaron means "of the four"). Another who willfully revised the New Testament was Lucian of Antioch (c. 240-312 C.E.). Lucian produced the Syrian text, renamed the Byzantine text. About 290 C.E. some of his associates made various subsequent alterations, deliberately combining elements from earlier types of text, and this text was adopted about 380 C.E. At Constantinople it became the predominant form of the New Testament throughout the Greek-speaking world. The text was also edited, with parallel accounts harmonized, grammar corrected, and abrupt transitions modified to produce a smooth text. As a result, this was not a faithfully accurate copy. However, others willfully altered the text to have it support their doctrinal position. Marcion (c. 85-c. 160 C.E.), a semi-Gnostic of the second century C.E., is a leading example. In fact, the idea of forming a catalog of authoritative Christian writings did not come to mind until Marcion. One such catalog was the Muratorian Fragment, Italy (170 C.E.) The list shows 24 books of the New Testament being accepted without question as Scriptural and canonical, some uncertainty about 2 Peter, and Hebrews and James were not listed, possibly unknown. In the end, we must admit that there were heretics who altered the text to make it align with their doctrinal positions, but also Orthodox Christians who also altered the text to strengthen their doctrinal positions.

We must keep in mind that we are dealing with an oral society. Therefore, the apostles, who had spent three and a half years with Jesus, first published the Good News orally. The teachers within the newly founded Christian congregations would repeat this information until it was memorized. Thereafter, those who had heard this gospel would, in turn, share it with others (Acts 2:42, Gal 6:6). In time, they would see the need for a written record so Matthew, Luke, Mark, and John would pen the Gospels, and other types of New Testament books would be written by Paul, James, Peter, and Jude. We can see from the first four verses of Luke that **Theophilus*** was being given a written record of what he had already been taught orally. In verse 4, Luke says to Theophilus, "[My purpose is] that you may know the exact truth about the things you have been taught."

* **Theophilus** means "friend of God," was the person to whom the books of Luke and Acts were written (Lu 1:3; Ac 1:1). Theophilus was called "most excellent," which may suggest some position of high rank. On the other hand, it simply may be Luke offering an expression of respect. Theophilus had initially been orally taught about Jesus Christ and his ministry. Thereafter, it seems that the book of Acts, also by Luke, confirms that he did become a Christian. The Gospel of Luke was partially written to offer Theophilus assurances of the certainty of what he had already learned by word of mouth.

The appearance of the written record did not mean the end of oral publication. Both oral and written would be used together. Most did not read the written records themselves, as they would hear them read in the congregational meetings by the lector. Paul and his letters came to be used in the same way as he traveled extensively but was just one man and could only be in one place at a time. It was not long before he took advantage of the fact that he could be in one place and dispatch letters to other locations through his traveling companions. These traveling companions would not only deliver the letters but would know the issues well enough to address questions that might be asked by the leaders of the congregation to which they had been dispatched. In summary, the first century saw the life and ministry of Jesus Christ, the Son of God, as well as his death, resurrection, and ascension. After that, his disciples spread this gospel orally for at least 15 years before Matthew penned his gospel. The written was used in conjunction with the oral message.

In the first-century C.E., the Bible books were being copied individually. In the late first century or the beginning of the second century, they began to be copied in groups. At first, it was the four gospels and then the book of Acts with the four gospels, as well as a collection of the Apostle Paul's writings. Each of the individual books of the New Testament were penned, edited, and published between 44 and 98 C.E. A group of the apostle Paul's letters, and the gospels were copied and published between 90 to 125 C.E. The entire 27 books of the New Testament were not published as a whole until about 290 to 340 C.E.

Thus, we have the 27 books of the New Testament that were penned individually in the second half of the first century. Each of these would have been copied and recopied throughout the first century. Copies of these copies would, of course, be made as well. Some of the earliest manuscripts that we now have indicate that a professional scribe copied them. Many of the other papyri provide evidence that a semi-professional hand-copied them, while most of these early papyri give evidence of being made by a copyist who was literate and experienced at making documents. Therefore, either literate or semi-professional copyists produced the vast majority of our early papyri, with some being made by professionals. The first-century Christians carried out their evangelism with a sense of urgency because the great apostasy was on the horizon, not so much that the end was nigh. So, yes, the spread of Christianity definitely had an impact on our efforts of ascertaining the original wording of the original text. Some facts that are found in THE TEXT OF THE NEW TESTAMENT are the early Christians were seeking to evangelize the world because of the foretold apostasy that was coming, they viewed the books of the twenty-seven New Testament books as inspired in the same way that the Jews viewed the thirty-nine Old Testament books as inspired, and, again, literate or semi-professional copyists produced the vast majority of our early papyri, with some being made by professionals.

CHAPTER 8 The Struggle for a More Accurate Text of the New Testament

When you open your Bible today, are you able to be confident that the words you are reading are in fact the very corresponding English words that were written by Matthew, Mark, Luke, John, Peter, Paul, James, and Jude nearly 2,000 years ago?

A world-renowned textual scholar of the 19th century, Dr. F. J. A. Hort believed this to be the case. Concerning the Greek New Testament, he wrote, "The amount of what can in any sense be called substantial variation is but a small fraction ... and can hardly form more than a thousandth part of the entire text."[76] The good news is, since the publication of his book in 1882, we have had manuscript discoveries that have far exceeded the value of any manuscripts that Hort had at that time. Continual research since then has confirmed that are New Testament Greek critical text today is a mirror-like reflection of what the authors at penned some 2000 years ago.

However, many Christians who hold their bibles in their hand each Sunday at church have no idea of the long battle that took place an order to obtain such an accurate, critical text that we possess today in the form of the Nestle-Aland (28ᵗʰ ed.) Greek New Testament and the United Bible Societies Greek New Testament (5ᵗʰ ed.). One textual scholar who was involved in this long battle for the Bible was **Johann Jakob Wettstein (1693-1754)**. Let us take but a moment to consider how he played his part in our struggle to have a more accurate text to the New Testament.

---

[76] B. F. Westcott and F. J. A. Hort, *Introduction to the New Testament in the Original Greek* (New York: Harper and Brothers, 1882), 2.

Wetstein was born in Basel, Switzerland. He was a Protestant Swiss New Testament theologian. A relative, Johann Wettstein, who was the university librarian, gave him permission to examine the manuscripts. He spent many long hours in the University library, as he was extremely fascinated by the Bible manuscripts. However, immediately it caught his attention that the manuscripts contained different readings. Therefore, Hey decided that he was going to base his theses for appointment as a minister on the subject of textual criticism.

Let's jump back a couple of centuries before to Basel, Switzerland, Erasmus was about to be hassled by the printer Johannes Froben. Froben was alerted that Cardinal Ximenes of Toledo, Spain, had been putting together a Greek and Latin Testament in 1514. However, he was delaying publication until he had the whole Bible completed. The first printed Greek critical text would have set the standard, with the other being all but ignored. Erasmus published his first edition in 1516, while the Complutensian Polyglot (many languages) was not issued until 1522

The fact that Erasmus was rushed to no end resulted in a Greek text that contained hundreds of typographical errors alone.[77] Textual scholar Scrivener once stated: '[It] is in that respect the most faulty book I know,' (Scrivener 1894, 185) This comment does not even take into consideration the blatant interpolations (insert readings) into the text that were not part of the original. Erasmus was not lost to the typographical errors, which corrected a good many in later editions. This did not include the textual errors. It was his second edition of 1519 that was used by Martin Luther in his German translation and William Tyndale's English translation. This is exactly what Erasmus wanted, writing the following in that edition's preface: "I would have these words translated into all languages. . . . I long for the ploughboy to sing them to himself as he follows his plough."

Sadly, the continuous reproduction of this debased Greek New Testament, gave rise to it becoming the standard, being called the Textus Receptus (Received Text), taking over 400 years before it was dethroned by the critical Text of B. F. Westcott and F. J. A. Hort in 1881. Regardless of its imperfection, the Erasmus critical edition began the all-important work of textual criticism, which has only brought about a better critical text, as well as more accurate Bible translations. The Textus Receptus had been venerated by the church as the received text for a couple centuries up until the days of Wettstein. On this Metzger writes, "The preface to the second edition [of Bonaventure and Abraham Elzevir (Erasmus' text)], which appearing in 1633, which appeared in 1633 makes the boast that 'the reader

---

[77] In fact, his copy of Revelation being incomplete, Erasmus simply retranslated the missing verses from the Latin Vulgate back into Greek.

82

has the] text now received by all, in which we give nothing changed or corrupted.' Thus, from what was from a more or less casual phrase advertising the edition ..., there arose the designation the 'Textus Receptus,' or commonly received text. Partly because of this catchword, the form of the Greek text incorporated in the editions of Stephanus, Beza, and the Elzevirs published exceeding in establishing itself as 'the only true text' of the New Testament and was slavishly reprinted in hundreds of subsequent editions. It lies as the basis of the King James Version and all the principal Protestant translations in the languages of Europe prior to 1881. So superstitious has been the reverence accorded the Textus Receptus that in some cases attempts to criticize it or amended it Have been regarded akin to sacrilege. Yet, its textual basis is essentially a handful of late haphazardly collected minuscule manuscripts, and in a dozen passages It's renderings are supported by no known Greek witnesses." (Metzger & Ehrman, 1964, 1968, 1992, 2005, p. p. 152) Metzger adds more insight,

So much in demand was Erasmus's Greek Testament that the first edition was soon exhausted and a second was called for. It was this second edition of 1519, in which some (but not nearly all) of the many typographical blunders of the first edition had been corrected, that Martin Luther and William Tyndale used as the basis of their translations of the New Testament into German (1522) and into English (1525).

In the years following many other editors and printers issued a variety of editions of the Greek Testament, all of which reproduced more or less the same type of text, namely that preserved in the later Byzantine manuscripts. Even when it happened that an editor had access to older manuscripts—as when Theodore Beza, the friend and successor of Calvin at Geneva, acquired the fifth-century manuscript that goes under his name today, as well as the sixth-century codex Claromontanus— he made relatively little use of them, for they deviated too far from the form of text that had become standard in the later copies.

Noteworthy early editions of the Greek New Testament include two issued by Robert Etienne (commonly known under the Latin form of his name, Stephanus), the famous Parisian printer who later moved to Geneva and threw in his lot with the Protestants of that city. In 1550 Stephanus published at Paris his third edition, the *editio Regia*, a magnificent folio edition. It is the first printed Greek Testament to contain a critical apparatus; on the inner margins of its pages Stephanus entered variant readings from fourteen Greek manuscripts, as well as readings from another printed edition, the Complutensian Polyglot. Stephanus's fourth edition (Geneva, 1551), which contains two Latin versions (the Vulgate and that of Erasmus), is noteworthy because in it for the first time the text of the New Testament was divided into numbered verses.

Theodore Beza published no fewer than nine editions of the Greek Testament between 1565 and 1604, and a tenth edition appeared posthumously in 1611. The importance of Beza's work lies in the extent to which his editions tended to popularize and stereotype what came to be called the Textus Receptus. The translators of the Authorized or King James Bible of 1611 made large use of Beza's editions of 1588–89 and 1598.

The term *Textus Receptus*, as applied to the text of the New Testament, originated in an expression used by Bonaventura and Abraham Elzevir (Elzevier), who were printers in Leiden. The preface to their second edition of the Greek Testament (1633) contains the sentence: *Textum ergo habes, nunc ab omnibus receptum, in quo nihil immutatum aut corruptum damus*("Therefore you [dear reader] have the text now received by all, in which we give nothing changed or corrupted"). In one sense this proud claim of the Elzevirs on behalf of their edition seemed to be justified, for their edition was, in most respects, not different from the approximately 160 other editions of the printed Greek Testament that had been issued since Erasmus's first published edition of 1516. In a more precise sense, however, the Byzantine form of the Greek text, reproduced in all early printed editions, was disfigured, as was mentioned above, by the accumulation over the centuries of myriads of scribal alterations, many of minor significance but some of considerable consequence.

It was the corrupt Byzantine form of text that provided the basis for almost all translations of the New Testament into modern languages down to the nineteenth century. During the eighteenth-century scholars assembled a great amount of information from many Greek manuscripts, as well as from versional and patristic witnesses. But, except for three or four editors who timidly corrected some of the more blatant errors of the Textus Receptus, this debased form of the New Testament text was reprinted in edition after edition. It was only in the first part of the nineteenth century (1831) that a German classical scholar, Karl Lachmann, ventured to apply to the New Testament the criteria that he had used in editing texts of the classics.

Subsequently other critical editions appeared, including those prepared by Constantin von Tischendorf, whose eighth edition (1869–72) remains a monumental thesaurus of variant readings, and the influential edition prepared by two Cambridge scholars, B. F. Westcott and F. J. A. Hort (1881). It is the latter edition that was taken as the basis for the present United Bible Societies' edition. During the twentieth century, with the discovery of several New Testament manuscripts much older than any that had hitherto been available, it has become possible to produce editions of the New Testament that approximate ever more closely to what is regarded as the wording of the original documents.[78]

Returning to **Johann Jakob Wettstein** (1693-1754), we find him spending long hours in the University library. His being aware that the manuscripts contain different readings was an act of bravery on his part when he spoke out in the thesis, attacking those who made the claim that any textual scholar attempting to alter the existing text of the Greek New Testament (i.e., the Textus Receptus, that is, the Received Text) was tampering with the Word of God.

Before taking up his appointment as a minister, Wettstein asked for time to travel. He had the idea and the hope of examining as many Bible manuscripts as he possibly could. So, in 1714 he set out on his journey, visiting Zurich, Geneva, Paris, London, Oxford, Cambridge, Leiden, and Heidelberg. Wettstein made complete collations (namely, a critical comparison, recording the differences), frequently for the first time, of the most outstanding Greek and Latin manuscripts of his day of the Bible. Richard Bentley of the University of Cambridge made his acquaintance in 1716; where he took a great interest and his work, at which point he persuaded Wettstein to return to Paris so they could carefully collate the Codex Ephraemi, as Bentley at this time had in mind a critical edition of the Greek New Testament.

In 1751, textual scholar Johann Jakob Wettstein was aware of only twenty-three uncial codices of the Greek New Testament. A little over 100 years later, in 1859, renowned textual scholar Constantin von Tischendorf (1815-1874) had brought the number of uncial codices to sixty-four. Some sixty years later, in 1909, Caspar René Gregory (1846-1917) identified 161 uncial codices. Some 210 years from Wettstein, in 1963, Kurt Aland (1915-1994) increased the count to 250 uncial codices. In the 1989, second edition

---

[78] Bruce Manning Metzger, United Bible Societies, *A Textual Commentary on the Greek New Testament, Second Edition a Companion Volume to the United Bible Societies' Greek New Testament (4th Rev. Ed.)* (London; New York: United Bible Societies, 1994), xxii–xxiv.

of Kurt and Barbara Alands publication *The Text of the New Testament*, the authors listed 299 uncial codices.

Wettstein gave us one of the modern methods of classifying these uncial codices. He used the Latin capital letters to identify the uncials. For example, Codex Alexandrinus was given the letter "A," Codex Vaticanus was designated "B," with Codex Ephraemi being given the designation "C," and Codex Bezae was classified with "D." The last letter to be used by Wettstein in the classification uncial codices was "O." As time passed, the number of uncial manuscripts became larger than the Latin alphabet, so future textual scholars exhausted the Greek and Hebrew alphabets. It was Caspar René Gregory who moved on to assign manuscripts numerals that began with an initial 0. Codex Sinaiticus received the number 01, Alexandrinus received 02; Vaticanus was given 03, Ephraemi was designated with 04, and Bezae received the number 05, to mention just a few. By the time of Gregory's death in 1917, the number had reached 0161, with Ernst von Dobschütz increasing the number of uncials codices to 0208 by 1993. As of June 1, 2010, the number of codices had reached 0323 in the Gregory-Aland system, a forgotten 4th– or 5th-century Greek fragment of the Gospel of John in the Syrus Sinaiticus,[79] dating paleographically to 300-499 C.E., cataloged by the Institute for New Testament Textual Research (INTF) in Münster, Germany.[80]

Wettstein Research Causes Problems

Wettstein was examining the Alexandrine Manuscript in London. **Codex Alexandrinus (02, A)** contains a complete text of the New Testament, minus Matthew 1:1-25:6; John 6:50 -8:52; and 2 Corinthians 4:13-12:6, dating to about 400-440 C.E. Alexandrinus is one of the four Great uncial codices. It is one of the earliest and most complete uncial manuscripts, along with Sinaiticus and Vaticanus. It has a Byzantine text-type in Gospels, Alexandrian in the rest of the New Testament.[81] In his

---

[79] "That the famous Syrus Sinaiticus contains not only the Old Syriac Gospels, but also other palimpsest leaves, among them four leaves of a Greek codex of John's Gospel, is not a secret. Nevertheless, for 120 years, this Greek fragment, though probably contemporary with the great uncials, was not registered in any list of NT manuscripts and, as a result, completely neglected." – https://bibil.unil.ch/bibil/public/indexSimpleSearch.action

[80] Retrieved Monday, August 19, 2019

http://ntvmr.uni-muenster.de/liste/

[81] Codex Alexandrinus resided in Alexandria for a number of years, the city from which it received its name. Thereafter, in 1621, Patriarch Cyril Lucar took it to Constantinople. It would later be given to Charles I of England in 1627, which was too late for it to be used in the 1611 King James Version. In 1757, George II presented it to the National Library of the British Museum. Alexandrinus was the best manuscript in Britain until 1933, when the British

examination of examination the Alexandrine Manuscript. Wettstein made a shocking discovery. Up until that time, according to the Textus Receptus in the King James version of 1611 com first Timothy 316 was rendered "God was manifested (θεος εφανερωθη) in the flesh." And, of course, this rendering was reflected in most other Bible translations in use. However, to Wettstein surprise, he noticed that the Greek word translated God, which was abbreviated too ΘC, in Codex Alexandrinus (400-440 C.E.) had originally looked like the Greek word OC, which means "who." However, there was a horizontal stroke ΘC showing through slightly from the other side of the vellum page. Moreover, a later hand had added a line across the top, which had, in essence, turned the word OC ("who") into the nomen sacrum (sacred name) contraction ΘC ("God").

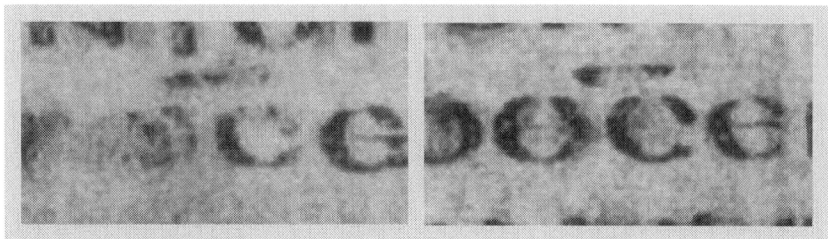

ΠΡΟΣ ΤΙΜΟΘΕΟΝ Α΄ 3:16 (WH NU) All modern-day translations

and confessedly great is the of the
16 καὶ ὁμολογουμένως μέγα ἐστὶν τὸ   τῆς

reverence well mystery; Who was manifested in flesh
εὐσεβείας   μυστήριον· Ὃς   ἐφανερώθη   ἐν ,σαρκί,

was vindicated in Spirit was seen to angels
ἐδικαιώθη   ἐν ,πνεύματι,   ὤφθη   ,ἀγγέλοις,

was preached in nations was believed in world
ἐκηρύχθη   ἐν ,ἔθνεσιν,   ἐπιστεύθη   ἐν ,κόσμῳ,

was taken up in glory.
ἀνελήμφθη   ἐν δόξῃ.

א* A* C* F G 33 Didymus

variant 1 ὃ εφανερωθη
"which was manifested"
D*

government purchased א for the British Museum for £100,000. Of possibly 820 original leaves of Alexandrinus, 773 have been preserved, 639 of the Old Testament and 134 of the New.

variant 2/TR θεος εφανερωθη
"God was manifested"
א^c A^c C^2 D^2 Ψ 1739 Maj

1 Timothy 3:16 King James Version	1 Timothy 3:16 Updated American Standard Version	1 Timothy 3:16 English Standard Version	1 Timothy 3:16 Christian Standard Bible
[16] ... God was manifest in the flesh, ...	[16] ... He was manifested in the flesh, ...	[16] ... He was manifested in the flesh, ...	[16] ... He was manifested in the flesh, ...

"who [or he who] was manifested in the flesh" was the original reading based on the earliest and best manuscripts (א* A* C*), as well as F G 33 Didymus. There are two other variant readings, "which" (D*) and "God" (א^c A^c C^2 D^2 Ψ 1739 Maj). Using Comfort's system, "A superscript c or numbers designate corrections made in the manuscript. An asterisk designates the original, pre-corrected reading." The witnesses (manuscripts) that support "who" or "he who" is very weighty. We can see from the above that there were many manuscripts that made what they perceived to be a correction in their manuscript, which clearly comes across as a scribal emendation. Certainly, the pronoun "who" is a reference to Jesus Christ.

$\overline{\text{ΚΣ}}$ for κυριος (Kurios) = Lord

$\overline{\text{ΙΗ}}$ or $\overline{\text{ΙΗΣ}}$ for ιησους (Iēsous) = Jesus

$\overline{\text{ΧΡ}}$ or $\overline{\text{ΧΣ}}$ or $\overline{\text{ΧΡΣ}}$ for χριστος (Christos) = Christ

$\overline{\text{ΘΣ}}$ for θεος (theos) = God

$\overline{\text{ΠΝΑ}}$ for πνευμα (pneuma) = Spirit

This simply solved textual issue caused many problems in the nineteenth century and really with the King James Version Onlyists, it still does today. The Bible scholars entered the fray because they thought the textual scholars were undermining their doctrinal position that God became man. The early argument by some textual scholars as to how the variant 2/TR came about was that the Greek word translated "God," which was abbreviated to the nomen sacrum[82] (sacred name) ΘC, had initially

---

[82] Retrieved Monday, August 19, 2019

https://christianpublishinghouse.co/2018/03/14/new-testament-textual-criticism-what-are-the-nomina-sacra-and-their-origin/

looked like the Greek word OC, which means "who" or "he who." They argued that a horizontal stroke showing faintly through from the other side of the vellum manuscript page, and a later hand added a line across the top, which turned the word OC ("who") into the nomen sacrum contraction ΘC ("God"). However, it seems highly unlikely as comforted commented: "how several fourth- and fifth-century scribes, who had seen thousands of nomina sacra, would have made this mistake." We would agree with Comfort that it was clearly a doctrinal motivation, wanting it to read, "God was manifest in the flesh."

Image 8 Codex Alexandrinus, 1 Timothy 3:16-4:3 theos

Metzger rates "He was manifested in the flesh" as certain, saying,

The reading which, on the basis of external evidence and transcriptional probability, best explains the rise of the others is ὅς. It is supported by the earliest and best uncials (א* A*vid C* Ggr) as well as by 33 365 442 2127 syrhmg. goth ethpp Origenlat Epiphanius Jerome Theodore Eutherius Cyril

Cyril^{acc. to Ps-Oecumenius} Liberatus. Furthermore, since the neuter relative pronoun ὅ must have arisen as a scribal correction of ὅς (to bring the relative into concord with μυστήριον), the witnesses that read ὅ (D* it^{d, ··} vg Ambrosiaster Marius Victorinus Hilary Pelagius Augustine) also indirectly presuppose ὅς as the earlier reading. The Textus Receptus reads θεός, with א^e (this corrector is of the twelfth century) A² C² D^c K L P Ψ 81 330 614 1739 *Byz Lect* Gregory-Nyssa Didymus Chrysostom Theodoret Euthalius and later Fathers. Thus, no uncial (in the first hand) earlier than the eighth or ninth century (Ψ) supports θεός; all ancient versions presuppose ὅς or ὅ; and no patristic writer prior to the last third of the fourth century testifies to the reading θεός. The reading θεός arose either (*a*) accidentally, through the misreading of ος as ΘΣ, or (*b*) deliberately, either to supply a substantive for the following six verbs, or, with less probability, to provide greater dogmatic precision.

Wettstein took notice of another interpolation that had entered into the text of the New Testament, 1 John 5:7-8. The King James Version reads, "For there are three that bear record in heaven, **the Father, the Word, and the Holy Ghost: and these three are one. And there are three that bear witness in earth**, the Spirit, and the water, and the blood: and these three agree in one." The words that are bold here, Wettstein had noticed they have been added to later manuscripts, or they were not found and any of the early Greek manuscripts that he had examined. With many other manuscripts now confirming Wettstein's readings, we now have far more accurate modern translations.

---

1 John 5:7-8 King James Version (KJV)

⁷ For there are three that bear record in heaven, the Father, the Word, and the Holy Ghost: and these three are one.

⁸ And there are three that bear witness in earth, the Spirit, and the water, and the blood: and these three agree in one

---

1 John 5:7-8 (UASV)	1 John 5:7-8 (ESV)	1 John 5:7-8 (CSB)
⁷ For there are three that testify: ⁸ the Spirit and the water and the blood; and the three are in agreement.	⁷ For there are three that testify:⁸ the Spirit and the water and the blood; and these three agree.	⁷ For there are three that testify: ⁸ the Spirit, the water, and the blood—and these three are in agreement.

A New Testament textual scholar is one who goes through the process of comparing all of the manuscripts of the New Testament in order to determine the original wording of the original text. Without the work of hundreds of textual scholars, including **Johann Jakob Wettstein** (1693-1754), we could not have an accurate text of the New Testament, which means that would not have accurate translations. Wettstein's work as a textual scholar has long been surpassed, overtaken by continual progress of hundreds of other textual scholars in the past 260 years, from Johann Jacob Griesbach (1745-1812), to Karl Lackmann (1793-1851), to Friedrich Constantin Von Tischendorf (1815-1974), to Brooke Foss Westcott (1825-1901) and Fenton John Anthony Hort (1828-1892), to Eberhard Nestle (1851-1913), to Erwin Nestle (1883-1972) to Kurt Aland (1915-1994) and Barbara Aland (1937-), and Bruce Manning Metzger (1914-2007). Trust me when I say this list could run for pages and many of those named here gave their entire lives to their work in textual criticism. Thus, Wettstein had a dream of one day of having an accurate text of the New Testament, which is now a reality. This text is not shaped by theological bias but rather, it has been constructed on sound textual principles. So, today when you pick up any literal translation except for the New American Standard Bible (NASB), which has retained the interpolations of the Textus Receptus for fear of losing sales to the King James Version readers, you can be confident that it has as its basis a text (NA 28th and UBS 5th) that truly presents us with the wording of the original text (99.99%) from which our Christian teachings can be derived. But only by studying the history of how the Greek text came down to us will you come to have the same respect for it that Wetstein had and be thoroughly convinced that it is the final authority, the inspired by, fully inerrant Word of God.

CHAPTER 9 Hundreds of Thousands of Mistakes Were Made In Copying the Greek New Testament Manuscripts

Was the purity of the Bible Text Threatened? Were these serious enough to ruin the Message of the Bible?

Dionysius of Corinth,[83] an avowed Christian overseer in the second century, lamented what had been done to his own writings. "For I wrote letters when the brethren requested me to write. And these letters the apostles of the devil have filled with tares [weeds, the sons of the wicked one], *taking away* some things and *adding* others, for whom a woe is in store. It is not wonderful, then, if *some have attempted to adulterate the Lord's writings* when they have formed designs against those which are not such."

The words of Dionysius show us that in his day (c. 71 C.E.) "*some have attempted to adulterate the Lord's writings,*" the Scriptures. Tertullian tells us of that same period, "Marcion expressly and openly used the knife, not the pen since he made such an excision of the Scriptures as suited his own subject-matter."[84] "That is, cutting out whatever did not fall in with it." (Dodgson)

---

[83] Retrieved Monday, August 19, 2019
https://christianpublishinghouse.co/2019/03/07/dionysius-of-corinth/

[84] Tertullian, "The Prescription against Heretics," in *Latin Christianity: Its Founder, Tertullian*, ed. Alexander Roberts, James Donaldson, and A. Cleveland Coxe, trans. Peter

Sadly, 30 years ago, almost all Christians would have been stunned if they had heard that there were intentional and unintentional changes made in the process of copying the manuscripts of the New Testament over a 1,400-year period, some 400,000+ variants. In fact, they would have been in denial, rejecting such an idea out of hand. The good news is, with the explosion of interest in Christian apologetics, evangelism, early Christianity, and textual criticism, there have been many dozens of books published on these subjects, and hundreds of thousands of Christians now understand and they fully realize that such purposeful tampering and accidental errors were not successful, changing the meaning of the Bible message because no one manuscript contained all of the textual errors, not even the master Greek text made up from the corrupt Byzantine manuscripts, that is, the Textus Receptus.[85] The fact is, there was no choice but to copy by hand for centuries because the Guttenberg printing press was not invented until 1455. However, again, the copyists did not destroy the purity of God's Word because (1) no text contains all the scribal errors, only a microscopic amount, (2) we have the original text within our 5,836 Greek New Testament manuscripts, (3) 400+ years of textual scholarship has given us a restored mirror-like reflection of the original Greek New Testament.

The Greek New Testament Manuscripts

We have the 27 books of the New Testament that were penned individually in the second half of the first century. Each of these would have been copied and recopied throughout the first century. Copies of these copies would, of course, be made as well. Some of the earliest manuscripts that we now have indicate that a professional scribe copied them. Many of the other papyri provide evidence that a semi-professional hand-copied them, while most of these early papyri give evidence of being made by a copyist who was literate and experienced at making documents. Therefore, either literate or semi-professional copyists produced the vast majority of our early papyri, with some being made by professionals.

The earliest sources for the Greek New Testament are the papyri in codex (book-like) form. Of course, this designation came from the medium on which they were inscribed. At present, there have been over one hundred of these discovered, with sixty-two of these manuscripts dating between 100 – 300 C.E. These biblical papyri range from a very small

---

Holmes, vol. 3, The Ante-Nicene Fathers (Buffalo, NY: Christian Literature Company, 1885), 262.

[85] Retrieved Monday, August 19, 2019

https://christianpublishinghouse.co/2019/03/09/desiderius-erasmus-and-the-textus-receptus/

fragment to codices, which may be incomplete, but still, contain large portions of several New Testament books. They are noted in literature with the Black letter character also known as Gothic script 𝔓, or by an upper- or lowercase "P" followed by a superscript Arabic number. (e.g., P^{52}, P^{66}, and P^{75}).

The Diocletian persecution (303-313 C.E.) was, in the end, unsuccessful. Many Christian libraries escaped the persecution of Diocletian. Two of the best collections today, the Beatty and Bodmer papyri, survived the fires. Alfred Chester Beatty (1875-1968), at the age of 32, had amassed a fortune. As a collector of books, he had over 50 papyrus codices, both religious and secular, which are dated earlier than the fourth century C.E. There are seven consisting of portions of Old Testament books, and three consisting of portions of the New Testament (P^{45} c. 250, P^{46} c. 175–225, and P^{47} c. 250-300). Martin Bodmer (1899-1971) was also a wealthy collector, who discovered twenty-two papyri in Egypt in 1952 which contained parts of the Old and New Testaments, as well as other early Christian literature. Particularly noteworthy are the New Testament Bodmer papyri, which consist of P^{66} dating to c. 200 C.E. and P^{75} dating to c. 175 C.E. Many in rural Egypt would have heard of the persecution in Alexandria, likely making great efforts to remove their manuscripts from their congregations, hiding them until the persecution was lifted. These early manuscripts and many others (such as Codex Vaticanus c. 300–325 C.E. and Codex Sinaiticus c. 330–360 C.E.) demonstrate extraordinary stability in the transmission history of the Greek New Testament text in the first 300 years.

Unlike the denial of the King James Onlyist (KJVO), Textus Receptus Onlyist (TRO), and Majority Text Onlyist (MTO), we accept the fact of 1,400 years of 400,000 copyist errors. Bible copyists made mistakes. However, none of those mistakes end up corrupting the Bible. Because we also accept the lifetime work of hundreds of New Testament textual scholars, who have restored the Greek New Testament to a mirror image of the original. We also accept the meticulous care of the Masoretes in their copying of the Hebrew text, which has given us the inspired Word of God, as they preserved textual integrity. Rather than having corrupted translations today, the tens of thousands of Old Testament and New Testament manuscripts have given us the Word of God in our language within the literal translations that are accurate in their rendering of the original language words.

The uniquely large number of New Testament manuscripts and their comparative proximity to the time of writing establish the textual reliability of the New Testament, including a 99%-plus fidelity to the divinely inspired New Testament as originally written. If you placed the manuscript copies of the average ancient author it would form a pile four feet high. However, the NT manuscripts and translations would reach a mile high. – Dr. Daniel Wallace is an American professor of New Testament Studies at Dallas Theological Seminary. He is also the founder and executive director of the Center for the Study of New Testament Manuscripts

The sheer volume of Greek New Testament manuscripts today actually helps Bible scholars to weed out the textual variants (errors). While Preservation of Scripture should never be equated with the inerrancy of Scripture, we can appreciate Preservation of Scripture by Restoration as getting us a reliable, accurate, and trustworthy text and a literal translation that has the equivalent of the original language words.

CHAPTER 10 How Did the Bible Survive Careless and Even Deceitful Copyists

Image 9 Scribe Hard at Work

Preservation of Scripture

This is one of the most hotly debated discussions, this new doctrine **Preservation of Scripture**. Some have equated this doctrine with Inerrancy of Scripture. Inerrancy of Scripture is simply that the original authors were inspired and that they were moved along by Holy Spirit so that the end product was, in essence, literally God's Word, with no mistakes, errors, and contradictions. Preservation of Scripture is best argued by John Burgon (1813–1888):

> There exists no reason for supposing that the Divine Agent, who in the first instance thus gave to mankind the Scriptures of Truth, straightway abdicated His office; took no further care of His work; abandoned those precious writings to their fate. That a perpetual miracle was wrought for their preservation—that copyists were protected against the risk of error, or evil men prevented from adulterating shamefully copies of the Deposit—

no one, it is presumed, is so weak as to suppose. But it is quite a different thing to claim that all down the ages the sacred writings must needs have been God's peculiar care; that the Church under Him has watched over them with intelligence and skill; has recognized which copies exhibit a fabricated, which an honestly transcribed text; has generally sanctioned the one, and generally disallowed the other. – John W. Burgon, The Traditional Text of the Gospels, ed. Edward Miller (London: George Bell and Sons, 1896), pp. 11–12.

When we look at those pushing this Preservation of Scripture, it is predominantly the King James Onlyist (KJVO), Textus Receptus Onlyist (TRO), and Majority Text Onlyist (MTO), it soon becomes apparent that the doctrine of the Preservation of Scripture is really no doctrine at all. We should note that there is no translation based on the Majority Text.

King James Onlyist (KJVO): Of course, the New Testament of the King James Version is based on the Textus Receptus. Both the King James Onlyist (KJVO) and the Textus Receptus Onlyist (TRO) are of the same mind, the same way of thinking. The King James Onlyist are that the King James Version is the only English Bible that should be viewed as God's Word.

Textus Receptus Onlyist (TRO): These scholars and their followers believe that the critical Text of Erasmus of 1516, the 1550 Stephanus New Testament, and all the critical New Testament Texts up until 1633 better preserve the original. While the Textus Receptus is based on the Byzantine text, it is only based on about seven manuscripts out of thousands. Daniel B. Wallace has counted 1,838 differences between the Textus Receptus and the Majority Text of Hodges and Farstad. – "Some Second Thoughts on the Majority Text," Bibliotheca Sacra 146 (July–September 1989): 276.)

Majority Text Onlyist (MTO): These scholars and their followers believe that the words penned by the original authors are better preserved in the thousands of Byzantine texts.

We do not have time to delve deeply into these scholars or and those who hold their beliefs. Please consider THE PRESERVATION OF SCRIPTURE.[86] Let us just say that we cannot have both 400,000+ textual variants (errors) in the 5,836 Greek New Testament manuscripts and the Preservation of scripture too as the King James Onlyist (KJVO), Textus Receptus Onlyist (TRO), and the Majority Text Onlyist (MTO) would contend.

---

[86] Retrieved Monday, August 19, 2019

https://christianpublishinghouse.files.wordpress.com/2019/01/the-preservation-of-scripture.pdf

If the Word of God is preserved (Preservation of Scripture), why does every single manuscript read differently in the Greek NT manuscripts, with hundreds of thousands of textual variants? You cannot have preservation alone; it needs to be qualified. PRESERVATION BY RESTORATION. Following the corruption person of 1,400 years of copying by hand is a period of 600 years of restoration by hundreds of textual scholars who gave their lives so that we now have a mirror-like image of what the original authors penned.

Isaiah 40:8 Updated American Standard Version (UASV)

[8] The grass withers, the flower fades,
but the word of our God will stand forever.

God had promised that he would preserve his Word, the Bible. The apostle Peter quoted Isaiah 40:6, 8. For, "All flesh is like grass, And all its glory like the flower of grass. The grass withers, And the flower falls off, But the word of the Lord endures forever." And this is the word which was preached to you as good news." (1 Peter 1:24-25.) However, we must consider Satan, the enemy of God, who has likely played a significant role in attempting to corrupt it and destroy it. (Matthew 13:39) Nevertheless, what we have today is a mirror-like reflection of what was penned and published by the original authors. So, yes what we have a **Preservation of Scripture by Restoration**.

It should be stated that some Bible copyists were careless, even deceitful. Paleographers have set out four basic levels of handwriting. First, there was the *common hand* of a person who was untrained in making copies. Second, there was the documentary hand of an individual who was trained in preparing documents. The third level was the *reformed documentary* hand of a copyist who was experienced in the preparation of documents and copying literature; and fourth was the *professional hand*, the scribe experienced in producing literature.

We have the 27 books of the New Testament that were penned individually in the second half of the first century. Each of these would have been copied and recopied throughout the first century. Copies of these copies would, of course, be made as well. Some of the earliest manuscripts that we now have indicate that a professional scribe copied them. Many of the other papyri provide evidence that a semi-professional hand copied them, while most of these early papyri give evidence of being made by a copyist who was literate and experienced at making documents. Therefore, either literate or semi-professional copyists produced the vast majority of our early papyri, with some being made by professionals.

CHAPTER 11 New Testament Textual Criticism and Modern Bible Translation

We cannot possibly consider all English Bible translations, so we have decided to evaluate the essentially literal translation (ESV), the optimally literal (HCSB/CSB) and the actual literal translations (UASV, NASB, NKJV). We have no choice but to look at the Dynamic equivalent translations New International Version and the New Revised Standard Version. Before we list the translations let us offer the reader a general overview.

There truly has been a renewed interest in the field of textual criticism, which had lain relatively dormant for several decades. What has contributed to this renewed interest? Several factors have contributed to the rehabilitated awareness: **the internet** has provided such tools as Yahoo and Google discussion boards, where scholars and laypersons alike can discuss the science and art of textual criticism. The internet has given the layperson many free websites that offer comprehensive information about textual criticism. **Evangelism** is another reason for the resurgence of textual criticism. Evangelism is defined as "planting the seeds of the Gospel" while Preevangelism is defined as *"tilling the soil of people's minds and hearts to help them be more willing to listen to the truth"* (Geisler and Geisler 2009, p. 22). This leads us to the third main reason for the renewed interest: The **New Atheist, Agnostic, and Skeptic,** who seek to cast doubt on the existence of God and his Word. These new critics of God and the Bible are different from those of 60 years ago or so, as they are far more evangelistic than even Christians. These new critics pen many books, magazine articles, advertising on billboards, news, and radio shows, and publicly debate Bible scholars. They seem to be everywhere and are contributing to the spiritual shipwreck of tens of thousands of Christians.

The fourth contributing factor to this renewed interest is **scholarly books written for the layperson,** which have enabled the churchgoer to enter the conversation. We now have a plethora of books dealing with numerous biblical fields, which enable Christians to avoid falling into the trap of doubting that what they have is, in fact, the Word of God, inspired and fully inerrant. There is absolutely no one to be blamed if we end up in repeated conversations that cast doubt on our beliefs and the Word of God, except ourselves. If the average Christian is going to be effective in his Preevangelism (apologetics) of helping those with receptive hearts to overcome the assault on God's Word, they need good Bible study tools.

In addition, the renewed interest of textual criticism brings up why it is important to all churchgoers who may simply own a few good English translations. What is the benefit of all Churchgoers knowing about textual criticism? First, we might all agree on two very important points as it relates to translation differences. Most churchgoers would agree that what they want in their Bible is what God had the original authors write translated into English (ASV, RSV, NASB, ESV, CSB, UASV), not some interpretive translation, not what a translator thinks God meant in its place. (NLT, NIV, TEV, CEV) The same holds true with textual criticism. Most churchgoers would agree that what they want in their Bible is what God had the original authors, who were moved along by Holy Spirit to write, namely, the inspired, inerrant Word of God (ASV, RSV, ESV, CSB, UASV), not the thousands of intentional and unintentional textual errors of copyists that crept into the text over 1,400 years of copying. (KJV, NKJV, NASB, and the DRV) The same holds true with textual criticism. So, our understanding of the foundations of, the basics of Bible translation philosophy and textual criticism can enable us to make the best choice when selecting a Bible translation.

Do we as Bible readers seeking what God had penned under inspiration want the King James Version or the New King James Version that is based on the text of the 16th century (TR), the corrupt Byzantine text-type represented in the great majority of Greek Manuscripts? Or, rather, do we want the up-to-date Bible translations that rely upon the modern critical text of Westcott and Hort, the Nestle-Aland and the United Bible Society, which departs from the Byzantine tradition (WHNU). The following are critical texts: the **TR** stands for **T**extus **R**eceptus text (1550), **WH** stands for **W**estcott and **H**ort text (1881), and **NU** stands for the **N**estle-Aland text (2011) and the **U**nited Bible Societies text (2015). If we want to make such choices, eyes wide open, we must fully understand how the Greek text came down to us.

Why are Jehovah's Witnesses so easily able to convert Christians over into their religion, by the millions. It is because the Christians, sadly are unaware, they have not taken in enough knowledge of God's Word, in short, they lack knowledge. Therefore, what the Jehovah's Witnesses teach sounds very good and very reasonable, and even very biblical to a person who lacks Bible knowledge. The same is true with this King James Version Onlist cult, who are able to hold millions of Christians under their influence because the Christian lacks an accurate knowledge (Gr. *epignosis*, used by Paul 21 times) of exactly how the Greek New Testament came down to us. Yes, there are some KJVOist out there who have a good measure of knowledge about the text of the New Testament but it is through the prism of the mind control of the KJVOist, who having impacted their thinking and their way of thinking, so any real evidence is dismissed out of hand or seen as mere trickery by those who have the accurate knowledge of the Greek text of the New Testament. This is how the Jehovah's Witnesses operate, sowing doubt about all others. Witnesses say that true Christianity is the whore of Babylon and the tool of Satan, to trust them is to trust Satan and deny the truth. The KJVOist do the same in saying that all translations other than the KJV are the product of Satan.

In addition, understanding textual criticism is the same as understand Bible translation philosophy in another way. Those choosing literal translation do so because they do not want a translator making interpretive choices for them. The churchgoer can use textual criticism for the very same reason, removing the textual scholar from the driver's seat so they can determine for themselves if a particular reading is original or not. As they read the Bible, the churchgoer encounters textual footnotes and they are left out of the discussion if they have no knowledge of textual studies.

There is both good news and bad news. The good news is that all of the major English translation gives the reader footnotes where there are major textual issues that will affect the translation. However, the bad news is, this footnote means very little in the grand scheme of things. Let's consider Matthew 6:13.

Matthew 6:13 (ESV)	Matthew 6:13 (CSB)	Matthew 6:13 (NASB)	Matthew 6:13 (NIV)
13 And lead us not into temptation, but deliver us from evil.[a] [a] some manuscripts add *For yours is the kingdom*	13 And do not bring us into temptation, but deliver us from the evil one.[b] [b] Or from evil; some later mss	13 'And do not lead us into temptation, but deliver us from evil. [b][For Yours is the kingdom and the power and the glory	13 And lead us not into temptation·[a] but deliver us from the evil one.[b]' [b] some late manuscripts

101

and the power and the glory, forever. Amen	add For yours is the kingdom and the power and the glory forever. Amen.	forever. Amen.'] [b] This clause not found in early mss	one, / for yours is the kingdom and the power and the glory forever. Amen.

Matthew 6:13 Updated American Standard Version (UASV)

13 And do not lead us into temptation, but deliver us from the wicked one.[1]

[1] Matthew 6:13 ends with "but deliver us from the wicked one." This is supported by the earliest and best manuscripts (א B D Z 0170 f1). Within the other extant manuscripts, there are six different additions to the end of Matthew 6:13, which is evidence against any addition at all. Within this footnote, we will deal with just one, which is found in the Textus Receptus and the King James Version, "for yours is the kingdom and the power and the glory forever, amen." (L W Δ Θ 0233 f13 33 Maj syr) These later manuscripts do not outweigh the earlier Alexandrian manuscripts (א B), the Western (D), and most Old Latin, as well as other (f1) text types, and the early commentaries on the Lord's prayer (Tertullian, Origen, Cyprian). It seems that the scribes were looking to conclude the Lord's Prayer with an uplifting message, or in the case of a couple additional support for the Trinity doctrine. "because yours is the kingdom of the Father and the Son and the Holy Spirit forever. Amen." (157 1253)

What do these textual footnotes in the ESV, CSB, NASB, and the NIV tell you about this interpolation? Basically, 'some late manuscripts added this doxology at the and of the end of the Lord's Prayer.' The NKJV is just the opposite by saying, "NU omits the rest of v. 13." The NASB is basically with the NKJV in that it has the textual interpolations in the main text of the Bible itself and a footnote that reads, "This clause not found in early mss." The reader has no way of knowing if it is true, they have no way of defending it when they talk with the KJVOist on social media. All they can say in response is, 'it is what my Bible says in a footnote.' The Updated American Standard Version footnote offers the reader far more.

King James Onlyist (KJVO): Of course, the New Testament of the King James Version and the New King James Version is based on the Textus Receptus. Both the King James Onlyist (KJVO) and the Textus Receptus Onlyist (TRO) are of the same mind, the same way of thinking. The King

James Onlyist are that the King James Version is the only English Bible that should be viewed as God's Word.

Textus Receptus Onlyist (TRO): These scholars and their followers believe that the critical Text of Erasmus of 1516, the 1550 Stephanus New Testament, and all the critical New Testament Texts up until 1633 better preserve the original. While the Textus Receptus is based on the Byzantine text, it is only based on about seven manuscripts out of thousands. Daniel B. Wallace has counted 1,838 differences between the Textus Receptus and the Majority Text of Hodges and Farstad. – "Some Second Thoughts on the Majority Text," Bibliotheca Sacra 146 (July–September 1989): 276.)

Majority Text Onlyist (MTO): These scholars and their followers believe that the words penned by the original authors are better preserved in the thousands of Byzantine texts.

Significant Editions of the Greek New Testament

[There are] four [major] editions of the Greek New Testament: (1) the Textus Receptus, (2) Westcott and Hort's *The New Testament in the Original Greek*, (3) the United Bible Societies' *Greek New Testament* (third and fourth editions), and (4) the Nestle-Aland *Novum Testamentum Graece* (twenty-sixth and twenty-seventh editions).

The Textus Receptus (TR)

The Textus Receptus (abbreviated TR in the commentary) has its roots in the early fourth century, when Lucian of Antioch produced a major recension of the New Testament (see Jerome's introduction to his Latin translation of the Gospels, PL 29:527c). This text is sometimes called "Syrian," because of its association with Antioch in Syria. Lucian's work was a definite recension (i.e., a purposely created edition), in contrast to the Alexandrian text-type (see appendix D). The Alexandrian scribes did some minimal editing, such as we would call copy editing. By contrast, the Syrian text is the result of a much larger endeavor; it is characterized by smoothness of language, which is achieved by the removal of obscurities and awkward grammatical constructions, and by the conflation of variant readings.

Lucian's text was produced prior to the Diocletian persecution (ca. 303), during which many copies of the New Testament were confiscated and destroyed. Not long after this period of devastation, Constantine came to power and recognized Christianity as a legal religion. There was, of course, a great need for copies of the New Testament to be made and distributed to churches throughout the Mediterranean world. It was at this time that Lucian's text began to be propagated by bishops going out

---

from Antioch to churches throughout the East. Lucian's text soon became standard in the Eastern Church. For century after century—from the sixth to the fourteenth—the great majority of Greek New Testament manuscripts were produced in Byzantium, the capital of the Eastern Empire. All of these copies bore the same kind of text, one directly descended from Lucian's Syrian recension. When the first Greek New Testament was printed (ca. 1525), it was based on a Greek text that Erasmus had compiled using a few late Byzantine manuscripts (notably, minuscules 1 and 2 of the twelfth century). This text went through a few more revisions by Robert Stephanus and then by Theodore Beza. Beza's text was published by the Elzevir brothers in 1624, with a second edition in 1633. In this printing they announced that their edition contained "the text which is now received by all, in which we give nothing changed or corrupted." In this way, "textus receptus" (the "received text") became the name of this form of the Greek New Testament.

The edition of the Textus Receptus cited throughout [Christian Publishing House blog] is that of Stephanus (1550). The Elzevirs' text (1624) is virtually the same. Both can be called the Textus Receptus (TR).

In recent years, a few scholars have attempted to defend the validity of the Textus Receptus or what they would call the Majority Text. The Majority Text is nearly the same as the Textus Receptus, since TR was derived from manuscripts produced in Byzantium, where the majority of other Greek New Testaments were produced. The two terms are not completely synonymous, however, because TR did not attempt to reproduce the reading found in a statistical majority of witnesses. Thus, it does not consistently reflect the Majority Text throughout. Majority Text is more nearly synonymous with the Byzantine text-type because it was in Byzantium (and surrounding regions) that Lucian's recension was copied again and again in thousands of manuscripts.

Modern advocates of the superiority of the Majority Text over other text-types are Hodges and Farstad, who produced *The Greek New Testament according to the Majority Text*. Their arguments are more theological than textual. They reason that God would not have allowed a corrupt or inferior text to be found in the majority of manuscripts, while permitting a superior text to be hidden away in a few early manuscripts somewhere in the sands of Egypt. Further, they argue that the church's adoption of the Majority Text was a vindication of its correctness, while the obscurity of the Egyptian text was a sign of its rejection.

Most contemporary scholars contend that a minority of manuscripts—primarily the earliest ones—preserve the most authentic wording of the text. Those who defend the Majority Text (and its well-known incarnations, TR and KJV) would have to prove that these earlier manuscripts, usually having a slimmer text than what appears in later manuscripts, were purposefully trimmed at an early stage in the textual transmission. In other words, they would have to present good arguments as to why early scribes would have purposely excised the following passages: Matthew 5:44b; 6:13b; 16:2b–3; 17:21; 18:11; 20:16b, 22–23; 23:14; 27:35b; Mark 7:16; 9:44, 46; 11:26; 15:28; 16:8–20; Luke 4:4b; 9:54c–56; 11:2; 17:36; 22:43–44; 23:17, 34; John 5:3b–4; 7:53–8:11; Acts 8:37; 15:34; 24:6b–8a; 28:16b, 29; Romans 16:24; 1 John 5:6b–8a. Had these portions originally been in the text, there are no good explanations why they would have been eliminated. On the other hand, there are several good explanations why they were added, such as gospel harmonization, the insertion of oral traditions, and theological enhancements (see commentary on the above passages). It is true that some of the earliest scribes were prone to shorten their texts in the interest of readability, but these deletions usually involved only a few words. Thus, most scholars see TR as being the culmination of textual accretions.

Westcott and Hort, The New Testament in the Original Greek (WH)

Aided by the work of scholars such as Tregelles and Tischendorf, two British scholars, Brooke Westcott and Fenton Hort, worked together for twenty-eight years to produce an edition entitled *The New Testament in the Original Greek* (2 volumes, 1881–1882; abbreviated WH in the commentary). In this publication, they made known their theory (which was chiefly Hort's) that Codex Vaticanus and Codex Sinaiticus (along with a few other early manuscripts) represented a text that most closely replicated the original writing. This is the text, which they called the Neutral Text, that Westcott and Hort attempted to reproduce in their edition. Their work was historically significant in that it dethroned reliance on the Textus Receptus.

In my opinion, Westcott and Hort's edition is still to this day, even with so many more manuscript discoveries, a very close reproduction of the primitive text of the New Testament. Of course, like many others, I think they gave too much weight to Codex Vaticanus alone. This criticism aside, the Westcott and Hort text is extremely reliable. In my own studies of textual variants, in many instances where I would disagree with the wording in the NU edition in favor of a particular variant reading, I would later check with WH and realize that they had come to the same decision. This revealed to me that I was working on a similar methodological basis as they. Since the era of Westcott and Hort,

105

hundreds of other manuscripts have been discovered, notably the early papyri. Were Westcott and Hort alive today, they would be pleased to see that several of these papyri affirm their view that Codex Vaticanus and Codex Sinaiticus are reliable witnesses of a very primitive form of the Greek New Testament. They would have undoubtedly altered some of their textual choices based on the evidence of the papyri. For example, the testimony of $\mathfrak{P}^{75}$ (with ℵ and B) in several Lukan passages clearly indicates that Westcott and Hort were wrong to have excluded several passages in Luke 22–24 based on their theory of "Western noninterpolations."

The Nestle-Aland Novum Testamentum Graece (26th and 27th editions) and The United Bible Societies' Greek New Testament (3rd and 4th corrected editions) (NU)

In the [Christian Publishing House Blog] these two editions, which have the same text, are referred to jointly as NU; when it is necessary to refer to the volumes individually, the sigla NA[26], NA[27], NA[28], UBS[3], and UBS[4] UBS[5] are used.

The United Bible Societies prepared an edition of the *Greek New Testament* as a tool for their Bible translators, in which a full citation of witnesses was given in the critical apparatus for significant variants. After the United Bible Societies had published two editions of the *Greek New Testament*, they decided to unite with the work being done on the twenty-sixth edition of the Nestle-Aland text, a scholarly reference tool.

Thus, the United Bible Societies' third edition of the *Greek New Testament* and the Nestle-Aland twenty-sixth edition of *Novum Testament Graece* have the same text. Each, however, has different punctuation and a different critical apparatus. The United Bible Societies' text has a plenary listing of witnesses for select variation units; the Nestle-Aland text has a condensed listing of the manuscript evidence for almost all the variant-units. Both works have since gone into another edition (the fourth and twenty-seventh, respectively), manifesting a multitude of corrections to the critical apparatus but not to the wording of the text itself.

In *The Text of the New Testament*, Kurt and Barbara Aland argue that the Nestle-Aland text "comes closer to the original text of the New Testament than did Tischendorf or Westcott and Hort, not to mention von Soden" (1991, 32). And in several other passages they intimate that this text may very well be the original text. This is evident in Kurt Aland's defense (1979, 14) of NA[26] as the new "standard text":

The new "standard text" has passed the test of the early papyri and uncials. It corresponds, in fact, to the text of the early time.... At no place and at no time do we find readings here [in the earliest manuscripts] that require a change in the "standard text." If the investigation conducted here in all its brevity and compactness could be presented fully, the detailed apparatus accompanying each variant would convince the last doubter. A hundred years after Westcott-Hort, the goal of an edition of the New Testament "in the original Greek" seems to have been reached.... The desired goal appears now to have been attained, to offer the writings of the New Testament in the form of the text that comes nearest to that which, from the hand of their authors or redactors, they set out on their journey in the church of the first and second centuries.

Though the Alands should be commended for their work, it remains to be seen whether or not the Nestle-Aland text is the best replication of the original text. As noted before, I have my doubts. ... Nonetheless, the Nestle-Aland Greek text is now truly recognized as the standard text, accepted by most of the academic community as representing the best attempt at reconstructing the original text of the Greek New Testament.

Since the scholarly community worldwide is most familiar with NU, this is the edition given first in each listing of textual variants. The NU reading is printed as it stands in the UBS[4] edition, including accents. All the variants are unaccented, as in the critical apparatus of NA[27]. This presentation should not be interpreted as implying, however, that this text is "inspired" or infallible—as many scholars will readily attest. The NU editors were able to take into consideration the newly discovered documents as they sought to produce a more accurate text. In many places they no doubt have achieved their goal to produce a more accurate text than did Westcott and Hort. However, their strong reliance on the eclectic method has produced an uneven documentary text. In some, but not all, instances, the Nestle-Aland text presents an advance beyond Westcott and Hort.

Nonetheless, the reader will see that the NU and WH editions often agree on matters of major textual significance. Where the WH and NU diverge, however, NU far more frequently concurs with TR than does WH. Furthermore, where WH and NU differ, I am inclined quite frequently to agree with WH on the basis of documentary evidence.[87]

---

[87] Philip W. Comfort, *New Testament Text and Translation Commentary: Commentary on the Variant Readings of the Ancient New Testament Manuscripts and How They Relate to the Major English Translations* (Carol Stream, IL: Tyndale House Publishers, Inc., 2008), xxiii–xxvi.

Biblical illiteracy being at 90%+ and giving Christians a Bible written on a 9th-11th-grade level is not too effective.

UASV WILL ADD THESE FEATURES (Each one is 5-8 pages long)

Appendix A

- A1 Principles of Bible Translation

- A1 Basics of Biblical Interpretation

- A1 How to study the Bible

- A1 Basics of Old Testament Textual Criticism

- A1 Basics of New Testament Textual Criticism

- A1 Basics of Biblical Hebrew

- A1 Basics of Biblical Greek

- A1 Basics of Christian Apologetics

- A1 Bible Difficulties Explained

- A1 Basics of Biblical Archaeology

- A1 Basics of Christian evangelism

The ESV, CSB, NASB, and the NIV, as well as most other major translations, including the dynamic equivalent, do not provide the readers with what they need to be able to make an informed decision about these significant textual variants. These footnotes do not allow the reader a non-textual scholar to truly evaluate the different variants (textual errors) of a variant unit (place in the manuscript where there are multiple differences) because they do not know what internal and external evidence supports each variant, or how to evaluate the weight of these manuscripts behind the variants. If the reading in the main text has (א B P⁷⁵ and P⁶⁶) and the variant has (L W Δ Θ 0233 f¹³ 33 Maj syr), most churchgoers are going to think, wait, the variant has far more manuscript support than the reading in the main text, not knowing manuscripts are weighed not counted.

All the reader knows in the ESV, CSB, NASB, and the NIV, as well as most other major translations is that the Bible translation has made the decision for them, for they (1) do not have enough information in the footnote for them to evaluate the variants, and (2) if they were given external manuscript evidence, this would still prove to be unhelpful without knowing how to weigh the manuscript support. Moreover, how many churchgoers out of 2 billion can evaluate the variant readings for themselves by considering the internal evidence, such as context, style, and theological inferences. Thus, the reader is at the mercy of the translation's textual committee choosing for them. Think this through for a moment. The reader who has chosen a literal translation has done so because he did not want translators making interpretive choices for him. Now, we have the translation doing just that with the textual decision. If the reader had enough information by way of appendices Basics of Old Testament Textual Criticism and Basics of New Testament Textual Criticism, as well as a footnote that gave them the external manuscripts.

Romans 16:24 Updated American Standard Version

24 _____[1]

[1] P^{46} P^{61} א A B C 1739 It^b cop omit; DltVg^c, [The grace of our Lord Jesus Christ be with you all. Amen.], which is the same as the end of vs 20. The earliest MSS support the omission of this verse. All modern translation does not include this verse because of superior testimony.

Thus, what is the benefit knowing 'later manuscripts add this …' or 'early manuscripts do not contain this …'? Or, what is the benefit if the translation even listed the manuscript support if the reader cannot weigh the evidence himself for or against to determine for himself, which is the original reading?

The answer to our problem is quite simple for both internal and external evidence. There needs to be an appendix that makes the reader aware of how to weigh the manuscript evidence (Basics of Old Testament Textual Criticism and Basics of New Testament Textual Criticism) and a chart at the outset the translation that lists the major Manuscripts and Ancient Versions.

In summary, almost all modern translations of the New Testament use the Nestle-Aland-United Bible Society critical text that is reflective of the early Alexandrian family of texts. Nevertheless, these translations do offer the reader the briefest of footnotes that address the significant variants. At present, these footnotes do very little to offer the uninformed reader any means of weighing the evidence for or against a particular reading. Until this is made available in modern translations, readers are going to have to invest in a critical commentary that will enable them to hear reasoned arguments on most of the significant variant of the Greek New Testament, as to why one reading was chosen over another. The score below is based on whether the translation has textual footnotes, the detail of those notes, and is there any information provided so the reader can comprehend and make an informed decision about the footnotes.

Comparison Results by Score of to What Degree the Reader Is Informed about Textual Issues

Bible Version	Score	NT Textual Base
New King James Version (NKJV)	20%	Textus Receptus
New American Standard Bible (NASB)	30%	UBS5 & Nestle-Aland 28
English Standard Version (ESV)	30%	UBS5 & Nestle-Aland 28
Christian Standard Bible (CSB)	30%	UBS5 & Nestle-Aland 28
New Revised Standard Version (NRSV))	30%	UBS3 & Nestle-Aland 26
New International Version (NIV)	30%	UBS5 & Nestle-Aland 28
Updated American Standard Version (UASV)	100%	Westcott & Hort UBS5 & Nestle-Aland 28

American Standard Version (1901)—ASV

The ASV (essentially the same as the English Revised Version, 1881, with minor changes made for American readers) is the best English translation reflecting the Greek text produced by the end of nineteenth century through the labors of men like Tregelles, Tischendorf, Westcott, and Hort. These men were greatly influenced by Codex Sinaiticus and Codex Vaticanus, but not by the papyri, since only a few had been discovered and published by then. Thus, ASV reflects the influence of these two great uncial manuscripts and serves as a point of comparison with the subsequent twentieth-century versions. In this commentary, it is cited sparingly. – (Comfort, 2008, p. xxvii)

Revised Standard Version (1952)—RSV

The RSV is a revision of ASV. It was felt that ASV suffered from being too rigid; it needed reworking to make it more idiomatic. The demand for revision was strengthened by the discovery of several important biblical manuscripts in the 1930s and 1940s—namely, the Dead Sea Scrolls for the Old Testament and the Chester Beatty Papyri for the New Testament. The RSV New Testament was based on the seventeenth edition of the Nestle text (1941). (Comfort, 2008, p. xxvii)

Updated American Standard Version (UASV)

GREEK TEXT: The primary Greek text used for the preparation of the English text of the Greek Scripture portion of the Updated American Standard Version was the NA. Kurt Aland et al., Novum Testamentum Graece, 27th/28th Edition. (Stuttgart: Deutsche Bibelgesellschaft, 1993/2012).[88]

The Updated American Standard Version (UASV) holds to the classic literal translation philosophy of English Bible translations over the past five hundred years. The source of this philosophy was William Tyndale's New Testament of 1526; the King James Version of 1611 (KJV), the English Revised Version of 1885 (RV), and the foundation text for the UASV, the American Standard Version of 1901 (ASV).

The Updated American Standard Version endeavors to give its readers a deeper, more accurate translation that remains faithful to the original text. By translating Scripture into the closest possible corresponding modern English, the UASV allows readers to encounter God's Word at it was originally intended.

Developed by one Bible scholar, in the translation legacy of William Tyndale, the Updated American Standard Version remains faithful to the Bible's original text; therefore, the original author's meaning is never endangered for the sake of readability, for it is the reader's task to determine what the Bible author meant by the words that he used. In this literal translation that remains faithful to its translation philosophy, the reader can be secure in knowing that they are always getting the Word of God in English not what a translator has interpreted it to be. In order to achieve this, by way of the good judgment of the translator, every word

---

[88] Updated American Standard Version (Cambridge, Ohio: Christian Publishing House, coming 2020). https://www.uasvbible.org/

and phrase in the UASV has been considered against the original Hebrew, Aramaic, and Greek, to give its readers the fullest accuracy.

The UASV was produced using lexical or linguistic translation philosophy that focuses on the accuracy of translating from the original languages into modern English, painstakingly deciding what English word or phrase most closely corresponds to a given word of the original text, never sacrificing accuracy for the sake of readability. Almost always the translator has given the reader a literal translation, a word-for-word rendering, as it is clearly understandable. However, in the rarest of exceptions, if it has been determined that the rendering will be misunderstood or misinterpreted, there is no going to extremes in the literal translation of the text just for the sake of being literal. At times, the translator has retained the literal rendering, such as "slept" for example and added the phrase "in death," which completes the sense in the English text. (1 Kings 2:10) This process assures that the words of the original text chosen under inspiration by its authors are translated as accurately as possible for our readers.

New Revised Standard Version (NRSV)

For the New Testament the Committee has based its work on the most recent edition of the *Greek New Testament*, prepared by an interconfessional and international committee and published by the United Bible Societies (1966; 3rd ed. corrected, 1983; information concerning changes to be introduced into the critical apparatus of the forthcoming 4th edition was available to the Committee). As in that edition, double brackets are used to enclose a few passages that are generally regarded to be later additions to the text, but which we have retained because of their evident antiquity and their importance in the textual tradition. Only in very rare instances have we replaced the text of the punctuation of the Bible Societies' edition by an alternative that seemed to us to be superior. Here and there in the footnotes the phrase, "Other ancient authorities read," identifies alternative readings preserved by Greek manuscripts and early versions. In both Testaments, alternative renderings of the text are indicated by the word "Or."[89]

English Standard Version (ESV)

Similarly, in a few difficult cases in the New Testament, the ESV has followed a Greek text different from the text given preference in the UBS/Nestle-Aland 28th edition. Throughout, the translation team has benefited greatly from the massive textual resources that have become

---

[89] *The Holy Bible: New Revised Standard Version* (Nashville: Thomas Nelson Publishers, 1989).

readily available recently, from new insights into biblical laws and culture, and from current advances in Hebrew and Greek lexicography and grammatical understanding.[90] "In the end, its text lies somewhere between RSV and NRSV; the translators were less likely than the NRSV committee to change RSV readings in the direction of NA27/UBS4." (Comfort, 2008, p. xxviii)

Holman Christian Standard Bible (HCSB) / Christian Standard Bible (CSB)

The textual base for the New Testament [NT] is the Nestle-Aland *Novum Testamentum Graece*, 27th edition, and the United Bible Societies' *Greek New Testament*, 4th corrected edition. The text for the Old Testament [OT] is the *Biblia Hebraica Stuttgartensia*, 5th edition.

Where there are significant differences among Hebrew [Hb] and Aramaic [Aram] manuscripts of the OT or among Greek [Gk] manuscripts of the NT, the translators have followed what they believe is the original reading and have indicated the main alternative(s) in footnotes. The *HCSB* uses the traditional verse divisions found in most Protestant Bibles.[91] Comfort writes, "The Holman Christian Standard Bible was originally intended to be a fresh translation of the Majority Text; however, the textual basis was changed early on to the modern critical editions of the Hebrew Bible and Greek New Testament. In the New Testament, HCSB essentially follows NA[27]/UBS[4], although it frequently provides TR readings in the footnotes." – (Comfort, 2008, p. xxvi)

The 2017 Christian Standard Bible (CSB) In Its Own Words as to Trustworthiness

Below are two verses that I used for many principles in life, so let's use these verses for translation principles as well. We will use the 2017 Christian Standard Bible (CSB). My words are in the brackets, of course. Bold is mine.

But first, by way of explanation, **Dynamic equivalence** (CEV, TEV, NLT, NIV, TNIV) and formal **equivalence** (KJV, ASV, RSV, ESV, NASB, UASV), terms coined by Eugene Nida, are two dissimilar translation approaches (philosophies), achieving a differing level of literalness between the source text and the target text, as employed in biblical translation. The formal equivalence is faithful to the original language text and gives the reader the corresponding words in the English translation, so it is a lexical or linguistic interpretive translation philosophy. The dynamic equivalent

---

[90] The Holy Bible: English Standard Version (Wheaton, IL: Crossway Bibles, 2016).

[91] The Holy Bible: Holman Christian Standard Version. (Nashville: Holman Bible Publishers, 2009).

translation is faithful to the modern-day reader and goes beyond the literal translation into commentary interpretation levels.

Matthew 7:21-23 Christian Standard Bible (CSB)

[21] "Not everyone who says to me, 'Lord, Lord,' will enter the kingdom of heaven, but only the one who **does the will of** (bold mine) my Father in heaven.[22] On that day many will say to me, 'Lord, Lord, didn't we prophesy in your name, drive out demons in your name, and do many miracles in your name?'[23] Then I will announce to them, 'I never knew you. **Depart from me, you lawbreakers!**" (Bold CSB)

1 John 2:17 Christian Standard Bible (CSB)

[17] And the world with its lust is passing away, but the one who **does the will of** God remains forever. (Bold mine)

The reader should agree that the important point here is, what exactly is **the will** of the Father? Therefore, the actual Word of God is very important if we are to be doing **the will** of the Father and if a translator goes beyond a lexical or linguistic interpretation-translation over into the realm of interpretation-commentary, such as (CEV, GNT (TEV), NLT, etc.), he can give the reader the wrong meaning. Now, the ESV calls itself an essentially literal translation, so does that mean it is essentially the Word of God? Words matter.

The Updated American Standard Version's primary purpose is to give the Bible readers what God said by way of his human authors, not what a translator thinks God meant in its place.

The Updated American Standard Version's primary goal is to be accurate and faithful to the original text. The meaning of a word is the responsibility of the interpreter (i.e., reader), not the translator.

The Updated American Standard Version will be **one of the most** faithful and accurate translations to date. The CSB/HCSB, ESV, NASB, LEB are all great Bible translations that have many great strengths and some weaknesses. Below we will quote what the Christian Standard Bible says about itself and then analyze that point by point. Bold and different colors are mine.

CHRISTIAN STANDARD BIBLE VERSION INFORMATION: The Christian Standard Bible aims to draw readers into a deeper, more meaningful relationship with God. By **translating Scripture into the clearest possible modern English**, the CSB **allows readers to experience** God's Word at its fullest.

Developed by 100 scholars **from 17 denominations**, the Christian Standard Bible faithfully and accurately **captures the Bible's original meaning without compromising readability.**

The CSB was created using Optimal Equivalence, a translation philosophy that **balances linguistic precision to the original languages and readability in contemporary English.** In the many places throughout Scripture where a word-for-word rendering is clearly understandable, a literal translation is used. When a word-for-word rendering might obscure the meaning for a modern audience, a more dynamic translation is used. This process assures that both the words and thoughts contained in the original text are conveyed as accurately as possible **for today's readers.** (Bold mine)

QUOTE: By translating Scripture into the clearest possible modern English, the CSB allows readers to experience God's Word at its fullest.

RESPONSE: What does that mean, **the clearest possible English**? The dynamic equivalents have the clearest possible English because **clear** means being easy to perceive, understand, or interpret so the clearest, i.e., most clear of all would be the dynamic equivalents, such as the CEV, GNT (TEV), NLT, ERV, TNIV, and so on. However, being the **clearest** is not being the most accurate.

QUOTE: 100 scholars **from 17 denominations**

RESPONSE: This suggests that the translation will move away from what little literal translation philosophy that it has into the realms of an interfaith translation trying to please all people, such as the NRSV did.

QUOTE: The CSB was created using Optimal Equivalence, a translation philosophy that **balances linguistic precision to the original languages and readability in contemporary English.**

RESPONSE: Optimal Equivalence sounds like code for dynamic equivalence philosophy, not literal translation philosophy. The idea of balancing being accurate and faithful to the original language texts with the readability of the modern reader means that the translation committee is going to take over the job of the reader and determine what is readable. The meaning of a word is the responsibility of the interpreter (i.e., reader), not the translator. Bible readers need to be given what God said by way of his human authors, not what a translator thinks God meant in its place, so as to make it easier.

QUOTE: In the many **places throughout Scripture where a word-for-word rendering is clearly understandable,** a literal translation is used.

RESPONSE: This is a slippery slope and as each revision roles out, we will find the translation committee determining more and more what is **not** clearly understood. The bar is set far too low with the word **clearly** and **clearest** being used. We will understand this more so in our next quote.

QUOTE: When a word-for-word rendering might obscure the meaning for a modern audience, a more dynamic translation is used.

RESPONSE: The idea of **might obscure** is so dripping with subjectivity (based on or influenced by personal feelings, tastes, or opinions), it means that the most influential person on that translation committee is going to have the biggest impact. How about we drop the qualifier **might** and just go with **obscure**.

"The English Standard Version (ESV) is an "essentially literal" translation of the Bible in contemporary English. Created by a team of more than 100 leading evangelical scholars and pastors," which had William (Bill) Mounce as their chief translator, who also moved onto the translation committee of the New International Version. He is a serious advocate for the dynamic equivalent translation philosophy. I have inside knowledge that when the ESV committee wanted to stay with a literal rendering, many time Mounce overruled them, so the ESV became a far less literal translation. However, they have published several books that advocate literal translation over dynamic equivalent translations when they hired a DE advocate as their chief translator and abandoned the philosophy more than they should have. The same can be said of the well worded CSB information about itself.

QUOTE: This process assures that both the words and thoughts contained in the original text are conveyed as accurately as possible **for today's readers.**

RESPONSE: As can be seen throughout, the focus is not on being faithful to the original language text but rather on today's reader.

Why the Updated American standard Version (UASV)?

The translation of God's Word from the original languages of Hebrew, Aramaic, and Greek is a task unlike any other and should never be taken lightly. It carries with it the heaviest responsibility: the translator renders God's thoughts into a modern language. The **Updated American Standard Version (UASV)** is a literal translation. What does that mean?

Our primary purpose is to give the Bible readers what God said by way of his human authors, not what a translator thinks God meant in its place. – Truth Matters!

116

Our primary goal is to be accurate and faithful to the original text. The meaning of a word is the responsibility of the interpreter (i.e., reader), not the translator. – Translating Truth!

New American Standard Bible (NASB)

Greek Text: Consideration was given to the latest available manuscripts with a view to determining the best Greek text. In most instances, the 26th edition of Eberhard Nestle's *Novum Testamentum Graece* was followed.[92] It should be noted that the NASB includes the Textus Receptus readings found in the NKJV in the main part of the translation not in footnotes. Comfort writes, "this translation is clearly lacking in terms of textual fidelity: though it was originally supposed to follow the twenty-third edition of the Nestle text, it tends to follow the Textus Receptus." – (Comfort, 2008, p. xxviii)

New International Version (NIV)

The Greek text used in translating the New Testament is an eclectic one, based on the latest editions of the Nestle-Aland/United Bible Societies' Greek New Testament. The committee has made its choices among the variant readings in accordance with widely accepted principles of New Testament textual criticism. Footnotes call attention to places where uncertainty remains.[93] Comfort writes, "The New Testament essentially follows the United Bible Societies' first edition of the Greek New Testament (1966). It diverges from NA27/UBS4 in about 350 significant places—many in agreement with TR." – (Comfort, 2008, p. xxviii)

New King James Version (NKJV)

NKJV is a revision of KJV which modernizes its language but does not depart from KJV's textual decisions. The New Testament of NKJV is thus based on the Textus Receptus, with several marginal notes on readings in the Majority Text (noted in NKJV as M-Text; see discussion under "Textus Receptus" above). NKJV also lists many textual differences between TR and the text of NA26/UBS3 (noted as NU-Text or U-Text). The reader can thus note how many significant differences there are between the two texts.[94]

---

[92] New American Standard Bible: 1995 Update (La Habra, CA: The Lockman Foundation, 1995).

[93] The New International Version (Grand Rapids, MI: Zondervan, 2011).

[94] Philip W. Comfort, New Testament Text and Translation Commentary: Commentary on the Variant Readings of the Ancient New Testament Manuscripts and How They Relate to the Major English Translations (Carol Stream, IL: Tyndale House Publishers, Inc., 2008), xxvii.

CHAPTER 12 What Are Textual Variants [Scribal Errors] and How Many Are There?

The first part of this chapter will cover the gist of what is most often discussed in New Testament textual criticism today. Thereafter, we will discuss what should be the primary focus of NTTC (New Testament Textual Criticism). It would seem that Bart D. Ehrman and other Bible critics of his persuasion have sent many textual scholars on a quest. These scholars have become obsessed with discussing how many variants there are, how to count the textual variants, and whether they are significant or insignificant. Below, we will cover what is being said about variants, as well as whether some are more significant than others, and then close the chapter with what actually is the most important mission in NTTC.

Some Bible critics seem, to begin with the belief that, if the originals were inspired of God and fully inerrant, the subsequent copies must continue to be inerrant in order for the inerrancy of the originals to have value. They seem to be asking, "If only the originals were inspired, and the copies were not inspired, and we do not have the originals, how are we to be certain of any passage in Scripture?" In other words, God would never allow the inspired, inerrant Word to suffer copying errors. Why would he perform the miracle of inspiring the message to be fully inerrant and not continue with the miracle of inspiring the copyists throughout the centuries to keep it inerrant? First, we must acknowledge that God has not given us the specifics of every decision he has made in reference to humans. If we begin asking, "Why did God not do this or do that," where would it end? For example, why didn't God just produce the books himself, and miraculously deliver them to people as he gave the commandments to Moses? Instead of using humans, why did he not use angelic messengers to pen the message, or produce the message miraculously? God has chosen not to tell us why he did not move the copyists along with the Holy Spirit, so as to have perfect copies, and it remains an unknown. However, it should be noted that if we can restore the text to its original wording through the science of textual criticism, i.e. to an exact representation thereof, we have, in essence, the originals.

We do know that the Jewish copyists and later Christian copyists were not infallible as were the original writers. The Holy Spirit inspired the original writers, while the most that can be said about the copyists is that they were **guided** by the Holy Spirit. However, do we not have a treasure-load of evidence from centuries of copies, unlike ancient secular literature? Regardless of the recopying, do we not have the Bible in a reliable critical text and trustworthy translations, with both improving all the time? It was only inevitable that imperfect copyists, who were not under inspiration, would cause errors to creep into the text. However, the thousands of copies that we have enable textual scholars to identify and reject these errors. How?

For one thing, different copyists made different errors. Therefore, the textual scholar compares the work of different copyists. He is then able to identify their mistakes.

A Simple Example

Suppose 100 people were invited or hired to make a handwritten copy of Matthew's Gospel, with 18,345 words. Further suppose that these people fit in one of four categories as writers: (1) struggle to write and have no experience as a document makers; (2) skilled document makers (recorders of events, wills, business, certificates, etc.); (3) trained copyists of literature; and (4) the professional copyists. There is little doubt that these copyists would make some copying errors, even the professionals. However, it would be impossible that they would all make the same errors. If a trained textual scholar with many years of religious education, including textual studies, and decades of experience, were to compare the 100 documents carefully, he could identify the errors and restore the text to its original form, even if he had never seen that original.

The textual scholars of the last 250 years, especially the last 70 years have had over 5,800 Greek manuscripts at their disposal. A number of the manuscripts are portions dating to the second and third centuries C.E. Moreover, more manuscripts are always becoming known; technology is ever advancing, and improvements are always being made.

Hundreds of scholars throughout the last three centuries have produced what we might call a master text, by way of lifetimes of hard work and careful study. Are there places where we are not certain of the reading? Yes, of course. However, we are considering very infrequent places in the text of the Greek NT that contains about 138,020 words, which would be considered difficult in arriving at what the original reading was. In all these places the alternative readings are provided in the apparatus. Bible critics who exaggerate the extent of errors are misleading the public on several fronts. First, some copies are almost error-free and negate the critics, who claim, "We have only error-ridden copies."[95] Second, the vast majority of the Greek New Testament has no scribal errors. Third, textual scholarship can easily identify and correct the majority of the scribal errors. In addition, of the remaining errors, we can still say most are solved with satisfaction. Of the small number of scribal errors remaining, we can say that most are solved with some difficulty, and there remain very few errors of which textual scholarship continues to be uncertain about the original reading at this time.

400,000 to 500,000 Supposed Variants in the Manuscripts

With this abundance of evidence, what can we say about the total number of variants known today? Scholars differ significantly in their estimates—some say there are 200,000 variants known, some say 300,000, some say **400,000 or more!** We do not know for sure because, despite impressive developments in computer technology, no one has yet been able to count them all. Perhaps, as I indicated earlier, it is best simply to leave the matter in comparative terms. There are more variations among our manuscripts than there are words in the New Testament.[96]

Bart D. Ehrman has some favorite, unprofessional ways of describing the problems, which he stresses without qualification, in every interview he has for a lay audience or seminary students. Below are several, the first two from the quotation above:

- Scholars differ significantly in their estimates—some say there are 200,000 variants known, some say 300,000, some say **400,000 or more!**

- There are **more variations** among our manuscripts **than there are words** in the New Testament.

---

[95] (Bart D. Ehrman, Misquoting Jesus: The Story Behind Who Changed the Bible and Why 2005, 7)

[96] Ibid., 89-90

- We have only **error-ridden copies**, and the vast majority of these are centuries removed from the originals and different from them, evidently, in thousands of ways. (*Whose Word is It*, 7)

- We don't even have copies of the copies of the originals, or **copies of the copies of the copies of the originals**. (*Misquoting Jesus*, 10)

- **In the early Christian centuries, scribes were amateurs** and as such were more inclined to alter the texts they copied. (*Misquoting Jesus*, 98)

- **We could go on nearly forever** talking about specific places in which the texts of the New Testament came to be changed, either accidentally or intentionally. (*Misquoting Jesus*, 98)

- The Bible began to appear to me as a very **human book**. (*Misquoting Jesus*, 11)

Each of the bullet points above claimed by Ehrman can be categorized as an exaggeration, misinformation, misleading, or just a failure to be truthful. Many laypersons-churchgoers have been spiritually shipwrecked in their faith by such unexplained hype. What the uninformed person hears is that we can never get back to the originals or even close, that there are hundreds of thousands of significant variants that have so scarred the text, we no longer have the Word of God, and it is merely the word of man. How such a knowledgeable man cannot know the impact his words are having is beyond this author.

Miscounting Textual Variants

In 1963, Neil R. Lightfoot penned a book that has served to help over a million readers, *How We Got the Bible*. It has been revised two times since 1963, once in 1988, and again in 2003. There is a "miscalculation" in the book which has contributed to a misunderstanding in how textual variants are counted. In fact, there are several other books repeating it. A leading textual scholar, Daniel B. Wallace, has brought this to our attention in an article entitled, *The Number of Textual Variants an Evangelical Miscalculation*.[97] World-renowned Bible apologist Norman L. Geisler has commented on it as well.

Lightfoot wrote,

From one point of view, it may be said that there are 200,000 scribal errors in the manuscripts. Indeed, the number may well considerably exceed this and obviously will grow, as

---

[97] http://bible.org/article/number-textual-variants-evangelical-miscalculation

more and more manuscripts become known. However, it is wholly misleading and untrue to say that there are 200,000 errors in the text of the New Testament. (Actually, textual critics consciously avoid the word "error;" they prefer to speak of "textual variants.") This large number is gained by counting all the variations in all of the manuscripts (over 5,800). This means that if, for example, one word is misspelled in 4,000 different manuscripts, and it amounts to 4,000 "errors." Actually, in a case of this kind, only one slight error has been made, and it has been copied 4,000 times. But this is the procedure which is followed in arriving at the large number of 200,000 "errors."[98]

Wallace makes this observation in his article:

In other words, Lightfoot was claiming that textual variants are counted by the number of manuscripts that support such variants, rather than by the wording of the variants. This book has been widely influential in evangelical circles. I believe over a million copies of it have been sold. And this particular definition of textual variants has found its way into countless apologetic works." He goes on to clarify just what a textual variant is, "The problem is, the definition is wrong. Terribly wrong. A textual variant is simply any difference from a standard text (e.g., a printed text, a particular manuscript, etc.) that involves spelling, word order, omission, addition, substitution, or a total rewrite of the text. No textual critic defines a textual variant the way that Lightfoot and those who have followed him have done.

Geisler writes,

Some have estimated there are about 200,000 of them. First of all, these are not "errors" but variant readings, the vast majority of which are strictly grammatical. Second, these readings are spread throughout more than 5300 manuscripts, so that a variant spelling of one letter of one word in one verse in 2000 manuscripts is counted as 2000 "errors."[99]

Lightfoot evidently was thought to have erred by counting manuscripts, rather than the variants in the text. In fairness to Lightfoot, it should be pointed out that he deplored the system of counting "errors" by the number of manuscripts, as the quotation above reveals. He was simply saying that critics were doing this, not that it was proper. It is difficult to

---

[98] *How We Got the Bible* (Grand Rapids: Baker, 2003; p). Lightfoot says (53-54)

[99] *Baker Encyclopedia of Christian Apologetics*, by Norm Geisler (Grand Rapids: Baker, 1998; p. 532)

see why Wallace would attribute responsibility for the system to Lightfoot. Also, Wallace cited Lightfoot's 1963 edition that did not include the distinction between "error" and "textual variant."

Let me offer the reader an example for our purposes. First, we should underscore a few important points raised: 1) we have so many variants because we have so many manuscripts. 2) We do *not* count the manuscripts; we count the variants. 3) A variant is any portion of the text that exhibits variations in its reading between two or more different manuscripts. This is more precisely called a **variation unit**. It is important to distinguish variation units from variant readings. Variation units are the places in the text where manuscripts disagree, and each variation unit has at least two variant readings. Setting the limits and range of a variation unit is sometimes difficult or even controversial because some variant readings affect others nearby. Such variations may be considered individually, or as elements of a longer single reading.

We should also note that the terms "manuscript" and "witness" may appear to be used interchangeably in this context. Strictly speaking, "witness" (see below) only refers to the content of a given manuscript or fragment, so the witness predates the physical manuscript on which it is written to a greater or lesser extent. However, the only way to reference the "witness" is by referring to the manuscript or fragment that contains it. In this book, we have sometimes used the terminology "witness *of* x or y manuscript" to distinguish the content in this way.

We begin by choosing our "base" or "standard text." We are using the *standard text* (critical or master text), Nestle-Aland (NA) Greek Text (28th edition) and the United Bible Society (UBS) Greek Text (5th edition). These two critical texts are actually the same. Therefore,

Note: When the acronym **NU** is used, **N** stands for Nestle-Aland, the **U** for United Bible Societies, since the texts are the same. The apparatuses are different, the UBS version designed primarily for translators (more on this below).

In this writer's opinion, the critical NU text is as close as we can get to what the original would have been like.[100] Therefore, we can use the reading in the critical text as the original reading, and anything outside of

---

[100] It is true that some scholars, such as Philip Comfort, argue that the NU could be improved upon because in many cases it is too dependent on internal evidence, when the documentary evidence should be more of a consideration in choosing readings. It should be pointed out, however, that this is in only a relative handful of places, when one considers 138,020 words in the Greek New Testament, and it is hardly consequential. I would also mention that this writer would agree with Comfort in the matter of giving more weight to documentary evidence.

that in the manuscript history is a variant: spelling, word order, omission, addition, substitution, or a total rewrite of the text. Any difference in two different manuscripts is a variant, technically speaking.

Before going to our example, I want to emphasize that Bible critics, who grumble and repeat over and over again how there are 400,000 variants in the text of the New Testament, have only one agenda: they want to discredit the Word of God. They use the issue of variants as a misrepresented excuse for their having lost their faith, having shipwrecked their faith, or having had no faith from the start. These Bible critics are no different from the religious leaders Jesus dealt with in the first century. Jesus said of them, "Blind guides! You strain out a gnat, yet gulp down a camel!" (Matt. 23:24). They thrust aside 99.95 percent because 0.05 of one per cent is in not absolutely certain! Now let's turn to our example, which comes from the Apostle Paul's letter to the Colossians.

Example of a Textual Variant

Colossians 2:2 Updated American standard Version (UASV)

[2] that their hearts may be comforted, having been knit together in love, and into all riches of the full assurance of understanding, and that they may have a complete knowledge[101] of the mystery of **God**, namely **Christ**, [τοῦ θεοῦ Χριστοῦ; tou theou Christou]

See the chart below.

Variants	Variant	MSS or Versions
NU[102]	of the God of Christ	Standard Text
1	of the God	10 MSS[103]
2	of the Christ	1 MS
3	of the God who is Christ	4 MSS
4	of the God who is concerning Christ	2 MSS

---

[101] *Epignosis* is a strengthened or intensified form of *gnosis* (*epi*, meaning "additional"), meaning, "true," "real," "full," "complete" or "accurate," depending upon the context. Paul and Peter alone use *epignosis*.

[102] Recall that NU is an acronym for two critical manuscripts: (1) Nestle-Aland Greek Text (28th ed.) and (2) United Bible Societies Greek Text (5th ed.)

[103] This is only a partial list of the manuscripts, as we are just offering an example, to see how we count the variants.

5	Of the God in the Christ	2 MSS
6	of the God in the Christ Jesus	1 MS
7	of the God and Christ	1 MS
8	Of God the father Christ	4 MSS
9	Of God the father of Christ	5 MSS
10	Of God and Father of Christ	2 MSS
11	Of God father and of Christ	4 MSS
12	Of God father and of Christ Jesus	3 MSS
13	Of God father and of Lord of us Christ Jesus	2 MSS
14	Of God and father and of Christ	38 MSS
Total 14	14 Variants in 79 MSS	79 MSS

These variants are found in 79 MSS, Thus, we have 14 variants in 79 manuscripts, not 79 variants. We do not count manuscripts, as most textual scholars know. In trying to paint a picture about the trustworthiness of the text, this author does not think talking about variants is really helpful, and it can confuse the layperson. It is important for the churchgoer to know what a variant is and the general extent of the variants, but in the long run, it is the places in the text that are affected by variants that most matter, and what we have as our text in the end.

The United Bible Society's "A" "B" "C" and "D" ratings are fine, and the definitions by UBS, i.e., [A] **certain**, [B] **almost certain**, [C] **difficulty in deciding**, and [D] **great difficulty in arriving at**, are helpful but should be better qualified, with some numbers of what percentage of the text fall under each area.

All Variant Units (Places)

What we need to talk about is how many **places** there are where we find variants. What percentage is this of the entire New Testament text?

We can then discuss:

• What percentage of the text is untouched by variants?

125

- Of the percentage affected, how much can we say or surmise to be given an "A" rating, a "B" Rating, a "C," or "D" rating?

Variant Reading and Variation Unit

This section is based in large part on the work by Eldon Jay Epp and Gordon D. Fee, *Studies in the Theory and Method of New Testament Textual Criticism* (Grand Rapids, MI: Eerdmans, 1993), wherein Eldon J. Epp expands on the brief 1964 article of Ernest C. Colwell (1901–74) and Ernest W. Tune on "Variant Readings: Classification and Use."

Again, what we need to discuss is how many variation units (places) there are where we find variations. Before doing so, let us define some terms.

SIGNIFICANT AND INSIGNIFICANT READINGS AND OR VARIANTS: Below we have what are commonly described as significant and insignificant variants. *Significant* would mean any reading that has an impact on the transmission history of a variant unit. For example, it would apply to how we determine the relationship of the manuscripts to one another, such as where a particular manuscript would fall in the history and transmission of the manuscripts. It would also be impactful if the reading could help the textual scholar establish the original. Therefore, *insignificant* would mean just the opposite, referring to a reading that has very little to no impact at all in *many* aspects of a transmission history. The reason we stop at "many" aspects here is that all readings in a manuscript play a role in some aspects of the transmission history, such as the characteristics of the manuscript it is in and the scribal activity within that individual manuscript.

Insignificant—Nonsense Reading: As Epp points out, a nonsense reading is "a reading that fails to make sense because it cannot be construed grammatically, either in terms of grammatical/lexical form or in terms of grammatical structure, or because in some other way it lacks a recognizable meaning. Since authors and scribes do not produce nonsense intentionally, it is to be assumed (1) that nonsense readings resulted from errors in transmission, (2) that they, therefore, cannot represent either the original text or the intended text of any MS or alert scribe, and (3) that they do not aid in the process of discerning the relationships among MSS."[104] It should also be stated that the original did not contain any nonsense readings, as the writers were led by the Holy Spirit. The inspired author before

---

[104] Eldon Jay Epp and Gordon D. Fee, *Studies in the Theory and Method of New Testament Textual Criticism* (Grand Rapids, MI: Eerdmans, 1993), 58.

publication would have corrected any error by a scribe such as Tertius or Silvanus.

Insignificant—Certainty of Scribal Errors: while these errors "can be construed grammatically and make sense," there is a certainty on the part of textual scholars that these are scribal errors. These are not nonsense readings but rather readings that make sense, which are scribal errors beyond all reasonable doubt. These would "be certain instances of haplography and dittography, cases of harmonization with similar contexts, hearing errors producing a similar-sounding word, and the transposition of letters or words with a resultant change in meaning."[105] The problem that we sometimes encounter here is that what may be *certainty* of scribal error to one scholar may instead be an *almost certainty* to another, and even less so to another. The key element here in determining a reading that is understandable as insignificant is that it can be "demonstrated" so by the scholar making such a claim.

Insignificant—Incorrect Orthography (Greek for "correct writing"): this term is used loosely to refer to the spelling of words, which (for Greek) can include breathing and accent marks. Thus, one can refer to variations in the orthography of a word, or even to incorrect orthography. When a variation in orthography is due merely to dialectical or historical changes in spelling for variant readings, the variations are often ignored in the decision process because the reading in question is identical to another reading, once the orthographical differences are factored in (*mutatis mutandis*). Epp writes, "Mere orthographic differences, particularly itacisms and nu-movables (as well as abbreviations) are 'insignificant' as here defined; they cannot be utilized in any decisive way for establishing manuscript relationships, and they are not substantive in the search for the original text. Again, the exception might be the work of a slavish scribe, whose scrupulousness might be considered useful in tracing manuscript descent, but the pervasive character of itacism, for example, over wide areas and time-spans precludes the 'significance' of orthographic differences for this important text-critical task."[106]

Insignificant—Singular Readings: a singular reading is technically a variant reading that occurs only once in only one Greek manuscript and is therefore immediately suspect. There is some quibbling over this because critics who reject the Westcott and Hort position on the combination of 01 (Sinaiticus) and 03 (Vaticanus) might call a reading "nearly singular" if it has only the support of these two manuscripts. Moreover, it is understood that not all manuscripts are comparable. Thus, for example, one would

---

[105] Ibid. 58.

[106] Ibid. 58.

comfortably reject a reading found only in a single late manuscript, while many critics would not find it so easy to reject a reading supported uniquely by 03. Some also give more credit to singular readings that have additional support from versions. Singular readings that are insignificant would be nonsense readings, transcriptional errors, meaningless transpositions, and itacisms.

Significant Variants: a *significant* reading/variant is any reading that has an impact on any major facet of transmission history of a variant unit. One approach to identifying these is to remove the insignificant variants first: nonsense readings, determined (without doubt) scribal errors, incorrect orthography, and singular readings. Those readings that cannot be ruled out in this process are probably significant.

Number of Variants, Significant and Insignificant Variants vs. Level of Certainty

It would seem that some scholars have lost sight of the most important goal of textual criticism, namely, reconstructing the original. There is little doubt that agnostic Bible scholar Dr. Bart D. Ehrman has led the conversation on how many textual variants exist. The authors of this publication are focusing their attention on the initial goal of textual criticism, returning to the original. We believe that even now the Greek New Testament completely reliable. However, there are some 2,000 textual places within the New Testament that need to be dealt with because the witnesses and internal evidence require consideration and deliberation.

Level of Certainty

The level of certainty charts below is generated from A TEXTUAL COMMENTARY ON THE GREEK NEW TESTAMENT (Second Edition), A Companion Volume to the UNITED BIBLE SOCIETIES' GREEK NEW TESTAMENT (Fourth Revised Edition) by Bruce M. Metzger.

The letter {A} signifies that the text is certain.

The letter {B} indicates that the text is almost certain.

The letter {C} indicates that the Committee had difficulty in deciding which variant to place in the text.

The letter {D}, which occurs only rarely, indicates that the Committee had great difficulty in arriving at a decision. In fact, among the {D} decisions sometimes none of the variant readings commended itself as original, and therefore the only recourse was to print the least unsatisfactory reading.

The word count below is taken from the Nestle-Aland Novum Testamentum Graece using Logos Bible Software.[107] While this author has compiled the numbers regarding the level of certainty of readings from Metzger's Textual Commentary, he has not gone to the point of counting the letters or words at each variant place. We will just offer the reader the general statement that almost all textual variants in the commentary were based on a letter or a few letters in a Greek word, to two-three words. Seldom was it an entire sentence or verse, very rarely several verses like the long ending of Mark. Therefore, we have chosen three words as the average to multiply the total number of variants, so that the reader can see the truly small number of variants that are even worthy of consideration, as opposed to the total number of words in the New Testament. For example, Matthew has 18,346 words with a mere 153 places where we find variants selected for the GNT, affecting about 459 words.

We need to add and emphasize, that all of the variants counted were selected by the GNT editors as relevant for translation, and the total does not include other variant units that were not considered relevant for that purpose. A good number of these additional variants can be found in the NA apparatus, but only with considerable difficulty in many cases because the same variants are frequently handled differently in the GNT and NA apparatuses. The authors of this book do consider all variant units relevant even if a good number of them are difficult or virtually impossible to represent in translation (depending on the target language), and we recommend that the reader adjust the figures offered below by multiplying the numbers of variants by a factor of two, which should compensate for any variants that are not reported in the GNT text. We see no reason to assume a significantly different outcome in the ratings that might have been assigned to these variants if they had been included in the GNT, except possibly where no decisions might be possible in the cases of competing readings that were fully acceptable (rather than difficult).

For readers who have a working knowledge of NT Greek, it may be informative simply to select a few random pages of corresponding text from the GNT and NA and compare the apparatuses to see what is missing from the GNT relative to the NA apparatus. We believe that our suggestion of multiplying the variant figures below by a factor of two will appear more than reasonable; however, even using a factor of three or four will still leave a relatively minute percentage of "C" and "D" readings, as revealed below.

---

[107] Word Counts for Every Book of the Bible ..., http://overviewbible.com/word-counts-books-of-bible/ (accessed April 20, 2017).

So then, if we look at Matthew and first multiply the GNT variant units by three for an average three words a variant, we have 459 words. Of the 153 variant units found in Matthew, we are certain of about 32 of them, almost certain about 70, have a little difficulty deciding on 50, and great difficulty deciding on only one variant unit. When we say that we have difficulty deciding, this does not mean that we cannot decide, as we can. Moreover, a good translation will list the alternative reading in a footnote. So in the entirety of the Gospel of Matthew, there is only one variant place (Matt 23:26) which we would count as about three out of 18,346 words, where there was great difficulty in deciding the original. As it turns out, in this case, the GNT apparatus handles it as a variant of eight words, while NA breaks it into two variants, thus illustrating our point about the difficulty of comparing the two apparatuses. Some translations have incorporated the variant (ESV, NASB, NIV, TNIV, NJB, and the NLT), viewing it as the original, while other translations (NRSV, NEB, REB, NAB, CSB, and the UASV) see the variant as an addition taken from the previous verse.

Matthew 23:26 Blind Pharisee, cleanse first the inside of the cup,[108] so that the outside of it may also become clean. (UASV)

NU has καθάρισον πρῶτον τὸ ἐντὸς τοῦ ποτηρίου, ἵνα γένηται καὶ τὸ ἐκτὸς αὐτοῦ καθαρόν "first cleanse the **inside of the cup, that the outside** of it may also become clean," which is supported by D Θ f¹ itᵃ·ᵉ syrˢ (bold mine).

Variant/Byz WH καθαρισον πρωτον το εντος του ποτηριου και της παροψιδος ινα γενηται και το εκτος αυτων καθαρον have "first cleanse the **inside of the cup [and the dish], that the outside** of them may also become clean," which is supported by ℵ (B²) C L W 0102 0281 Maj.

Looking at the above support alone, it would seem that the witnesses for the longer reading ("and the dish") are weightier, making the longer reading the likely original. Then, when we consider the presence of a few manuscripts (B* f¹³ 28 *al*) that are not listed for the shorter reading because they have the longer reading ("and the dish"), the weight shifts over to the shorter reading's being the original. Why? Because these few manuscripts have the singular αυτου instead of αὐτῶν, even though they have the longer reading. This tells us that the archetype text was the shorter reading. Clearly, the copyist added ("and the dish") from the previous verse, Matthew 23:25, which reads, "Woe to you, scribes and Pharisees,

---

108 The NU (D Θ f¹ itᵃ·ᵉ syrˢ) has the above reading. A variant, WH and Byz (ℵ (B²) C L W 0102 0281 Maj) add "and of the dish." The variant is an addition taken from the previous verse.

hypocrites! because you cleanse the outside of the cup and of the dish, but inside they are full of greediness and self-indulgence."

Below, we will look at all of the numbers, the total words in the Greek New Testament, the number of A, B, C, and D variants in each book as they were selected by the GNT committee, followed by the total number of variants listed in Metzger's textual commentary.

The Entire New Testament (138,020 Words)

{A-D}	New Testament
{A}	505
{B}	523
{C}	354
{D}	10
Total Var.	1,392
Words	138,020

The Gospels (64,767 Words)

{A-D}	Matt	Mark	Luke	John
{A}	32	45	44	44
{B}	70	49	73	62
{C}	50	45	44	41
{D}	1	1	0	2
Total Var.	153	140	161	149
Words	18,346	11,304	19,482	15,635

The Acts of the Apostles (18,450 Words)

{A-D}	Acts
{A}	74
{B}	82
{C}	40
{D}	1

Total Var.	197
Words	18,450

Paul's Fourteen Epistles (37,361 Words)

{A-D}	Rom	1 Cor	2 Cor	Gal.	Eph.	Php	Col.
{A}	39	21	12	16	16	10	8
{B}	19	22	17	3	11	7	12
{C}	20	15	10	8	7	3	8
{D}	1	1	0	0	0	0	0
Total Var.	79	59	39	27	34	20	28
WORDS	7,111	6,830	4,477	2,230	2,422	1,629	1,582

{A-D}	1 Th	2 Th	1 Tim	2 Tim	Tit	Phm.	Heb.
{A}	9	3	15	2	2	2	20
{B}	2	3	2	6	1	3	11
{C}	3	2	2	1	1	0	12
{D}	0	0	0	0	0	0	0
Total Var.	14	8	19	9	4	5	43
WORDS	1,481	823	1,591	1,238	659	335	4,953

The General Epistles (7,591 Words)

{A-D}	Jam	1 Pet	2 Pet	1 Jn	2 Jn	3 Jn	Jude
{A}	7	21	8	18	4	1	9
{B}	12	9	7	7	1	1	0
{C}	4	7	6	4	0	0	3
{D}	0	0	1	0	0	0	1
Total Var.	23	37	22	29	5	2	13
WORDS	1,742	1,684	1,099	2,141	245	219	461

The Book of Revelation (9,851 Words)

{A-D}	Revelation
{A}	23
{B}	31
{C}	18
{D}	1
Total Var.	73
Words	9,851

As noted above, the authors of this publication maintain that all variation units or places where variations occur are significant because we are dealing with the Word of God, and reconstructing the original wording is of the utmost importance. Recall Lightfoot once more. "What about the significance of these variations? Are these variations immaterial or are they important? What bearing do they have on the New Testament message and on faith? To respond to these questions, it will be helpful to introduce three types of textual variations, classified in relation to their significance for our present New Testament text. 1. Trivial variations which are of no consequence to the text. 2. Substantial variations which are of no consequence to the text. 3. Substantial variations that have bearing on the text."[109]

Whether we are talking about the addition or omission of such words as "for," "and," and "the," or different forms of similar Greek words, differences in spelling, or the addition of a whole verse or even several verses, the importance lies **not** with the **significance of impact** on the meaning of the text but rather **the certainty** of the wording in the original. What we want to focus on is the certainty level of reconstructing every single word that Matthew, Mark, Luke, John, Paul, Peter, James, and Jude penned.

We will use Lightfoot's example of Matthew 11:10-23, that is, fourteen verses of 231 words; we have eleven variants in verses 10, 15, 16, 17, 18, 19(2), 20, 21, and 23(2). This may seem worrisome to the churchgoer or someone new to textual criticism. However, while all of the variants are found in the NA28 critical apparatus (2012), pp. 31–32,[110] the following sources below only covered seven of them because four are not even an issue. Why are they not an issue? We know what the original reading is with absolute certainty. The seven that have some uncertainty are mentioned in the textual commentaries below.

- Comfort *New Testament Text and Translation* covers verses 15 and 19

- Comfort *Commentary on the Manuscripts* and Text *of the New Testament* covers verses 12 and 19

- Metzger's *Textual Commentary on the Greek New Testament* covers 15, 17, 19, and 23.

---

[109] *How We Got the Bibles*, by Neil R. Lightfoot (Grand Rapids: Baker, 1998; p. 95-103)

[110] Eberhard Nestle and Erwin Nestle, *Nestle-Aland: NTG Apparatus Criticus*, ed. Barbara Aland et al., 28. revidierte Auflage. (Stuttgart: Deutsche Bibelgesellschaft, 2012), 31–32.

Immediately we need to note that verse 12 is absolutely certain as to the original words as well. Verse 19a is mentioned in Comfort's textual commentary because he is drawing attention to the "Son of Man" being written as a nomen sacrum ("sacred name" that is abbreviated) in two early manuscripts (א W), as well as in L. Therefore, verse 19a is absolutely certain as well. We are now down to five variants. The original readings of verses 15, 17, 19a and the two in verse 23 where variants occur are almost certain. The textual scholars on the committees for four leading semi-literal and literal translations (ESV, LEB, CSB, and the NASB) agree on ten of the eleven variants. There is disagreement on **Matthew 11:15**. Even so, the reader has access to the original and alternatives in the footnote.

"He who has ears to hear, let him hear." (ESV, NASB, UASV)

The variant is ο εχων ωτα ακουειν ακουετω "the one having ears to hear let him hear," which is supported by א C L W Z Θ f[1,13] 33 Maj syr[c,h,p] cop

"The one who has ears to hear, let him hear!" (LEB, cf. CSB)

WH and NU have ὁ ἔχων ὦτα ἀκουέτω "the one having ears let him hear," which is supported by B D 700 it[k] syr[s]

As is usually the case in more difficult decisions, the variant readings are divided in their support between the leading Alexandrian manuscripts. One reading has 01 (Sinaiticus) on its side, the other has 03 (Vaticanus). This tends to cancel out the weight of documentary evidence.

Now, we return to the charts above. There are 138,020 words in the New Testament. Just 1,392 textual variants deemed relevant for translation have enough of an issue to even be considered in the textual commentary. Again, if we average three words per variant, this amounts only to about 3.026 percent of the 138,020 words, or about 6 percent when we compensate for variant units ignored by the GNT editors. We can also remove the 505 {A} ratings because they are certain. Then, we really have no concerns about the {B} ratings because they are almost certain as well. This means that out of 138,020 words in the Greek New Testament, we only have 364 variants (1,092 words by our average) with which we have difficulty, a mere 10 of which involve great difficulty in deciding which reading to put in the text. Our average would make these variants 0.791 percent of the text without accounting for any difficult variants not included because they were considered irrelevant for translation.

We need not be disturbed or distracted by worries of how many variants there are, or whether they are significant or insignificant. We need only to deal with the certainty of each variation unit, endeavoring to determine the original reading. We should also be concerned with the role textual criticism plays in apologetics. There is no possibility of apologetics if we do not have an authoritative and true Word of God. J. Harold Greenlee was correct when he wrote, "Textual criticism is the basic study for the accurate knowledge of any text. New Testament textual criticism, therefore, is the basic biblical study, a prerequisite to all other biblical and theological work. Interpretation, systemization, and application of the teachings of the NT cannot be done until textual criticism has done at least some of its work."[111] We would add apologetics to that list for which textual criticism is a prerequisite. How are we to defend the Word of God as inspired, inerrant, true, and authoritative, if we do not know whether we even have the Word of God? Therefore, when Bible critics try to muddy the waters of truth with misinformation, it is up to the textual scholar to correct the Bible critic's misinformation.

Again, it is true that Lightfoot erred if he was counting the manuscripts instead of the variants. However, we need not count variants either but rather variation units, namely, the places where there are variations. The above Colossians 2:2 example of variations that are found in 79 manuscripts were seen to have 14 variants in 79 manuscripts, not 79 variants. While this is true, it is also true that this is simply one variation unit, i.e., one place, where a variation occurs. This may sound as though we are trying to rationalize a major problem of hundreds of thousands of variants. However, it is actually the other way around. The Bible critic is misrepresenting the facts, trying to talk about an issue without giving the reader or listener all of the facts. We need to consider Benjamin Disraeli's words on statistics: "There are three types of lies: lies, damn lies, and statistics."

The certainty of the Original Words of the Original Authors

Virgil (70-19 B.C.E.) wrote the *Aeneid* between 29 and 19 B.C.E. for which there are only five manuscripts dating to the fourth and fifth centuries C.E.[112] Jewish historian Josephus (37-100 C.E.) wrote *The Jewish Wars* about 75 C.E., for which we have nine complete manuscripts, seven of major importance dating from the tenth to the twelfth centuries C.E.[113] Tacitus (59-129 C.E.) wrote *Annals of Imperial Rome* sometime before 116

---

[111] *Introduction to New Testament Textual Criticism*, by J. Harold Greenlee (Peabody: Hendrickson Publishers, 1995; p. 7)

[112] Preface | Dickinson College Commentaries. (April 25, 2017) http://dcc.dickinson.edu/vergil-aeneid/manuscripts

[113] Honora Howell Chapman (Editor), Zuleika Rodgers (Editor), 2016, A *Companion to Josephus* (Blackwell Companions to the Ancient World), Wiley-Blackwell: p. 307.

C.E., a work considered vital to understanding the history of the Roman Empire during the first century, and we have only thirty-three manuscripts, two of the earliest that date 850 and 1050 C.E. Julius Caesar (100-44 B.C.E.) wrote his Gallic Wars between 51-46 B.C.E.,[114] which is a firsthand account in a third-person narrative of the war, of which we have 251 manuscripts dating between the ninth and fifteenth centuries.[115]

On the other hand, New Testament textual scholars have over 5,800 Greek manuscripts, not to mention ancient versions such as Latin, Coptic, Syriac, Armenian, Georgian, and Gothic, which number into the tens of thousands. We have many early and reliable manuscripts in Greek and the versions, a good number that cover almost the entire New Testament dating within 100 years of the originals. Therefore, reconstructing the original Greek New Testament is a realistic goal for Bible scholars. This belief and goal that we could anticipate a time when we would recover the original wording of the Greek New Testament had its greatest advocates in the nineteenth century, in Samuel Tregelles (1813-75), B. F. Westcott (1825-1901), and F. J. A. Hort (1828-92). While they acknowledged that we would never recover every word with absolute certainty, they knew that it was always the primary goal to come extremely close to the original. When we entered the twentieth century, there were two textual scholars who have since stood above all others, Kurt Aland and Bruce Metzger. These two men carried the same purpose with them, as they were instrumental in bringing us the Nestle-Aland and the United Bible Societies critical editions, which are at the foundation of almost all modern translations.

From the days of Johann Jacob Griesbach (1745-1812), to Constantin Von Tischendorf (1815-1874), to Samuel Prideaux Tregelles (1813-1875), to Fenton John Anthony Hort (1828-1892), to Kurt Aland (1915-1994), to Bruce M. Metzger (1914-2007),[116] we have been blessed with extraordinary

---

[114] Carolyn Hammond, 1996, Introduction to *The Gallic War*, Oxford University Press: p. xxxii.

Max Radin, 1918, The date of composition of Caesar's Gallic War, *Classical Philology* XIII: 283–300.

[115] O. Seel, 1961, *Bellum Gallicum*. (Bibl. Teubneriana.) Teubner, Leipzig.

W. Hering, 1987, *C. Iulii Caesaris commentarii rerum gestarum, Vol. I: Bellum Gallicum.*(Bibl. Teubneriana.) Teubner, Leipzig.

Virginia Brown, 1972, *The Textual Transmission of Caesar's Civil War*, Brill.

Caesar's Gallic war - Tim Mitchell. (April 25, 2017)
http://www.timmitchell.fr/blog/2012/04/12/gallic-war/

[116] These textual scholars provided us with histories of the transmission of the New Testament text and methodologies. However, we have had dozens of textual scholars who have given their lives to the text of the New Testament. To mention just a few, we have Brian Walton (1600-1661), John Fell (1625-1686), John Mill (1645-1707), Edward Wells (1667-

textual scholars. These scholars have devoted their entire lives to providing us the transmission of the New Testament text and the methodologies by which we can recover the original words of the New Testament authors. They did not construct these histories and methodologies from textbooks or in university classrooms. No, they spent decades upon decades in working with manuscripts and putting their methods of textual criticism into practice, as they provided us with one improved critical edition after another. As their knowledge grew, the number of manuscripts which they had to work with fortunately grew as well.

Samuel Tregelles stated that it was his purpose to restore the Greek New Testament text "as nearly as can be done on existing evidence."[117] B. F. Westcott and F. J. A. Hort declared that their goal was "to present exactly the original words of the New Testament, so far as they can now be determined from surviving documents."[118] Metzger said that the goal of textual criticism is "to ascertain from the divergent copies which form of the text should be regarded as most nearly conforming to the original."[119] Sadly, after centuries, textual criticism is losing its way, as new textual scholars have begun to set aside the goal of recovering and establishing the original wording of the Greek New Testament. They have little concern for the certainty of a reading as to whether it is the original.

In speaking of the positions of agnostic Bart D. Ehrman (author of *The Orthodox Corruption of Scripture*) and David Parker (author of *The Living Text of the Gospels*), Elliott overserved, "Both emphasize the living and therefore changing text of the New Testament and the needlessness and inappropriateness of trying to establish one immutable original text. The changeable text in all its variety is what we textual critics should be displaying."[120] Elliott then reflects further on his goals within textual criticism: "Despite my own published work in trying to prove the originality of the text in selected areas of textual variation ... I agree that the task of trying to establish the original words of the original authors with 100% certainty is impossible. More dominant in text critics' thinking now is the need to plot the changes in the history of the text. That certainly seemed

---

1727), Richard Bentley (1662-1742), Johann Albert Bengel (1687-1752), Johann Jacob Wettstein (1693-1754), Johann Salomo Semler (1725-1791), Johann Leonard Hug (1765-1846), Johann Martin Augustinus Scholz (1794-1852), Karl Lachmann (1793-1851), Erwin Nestle (1883-1972), Allen Wikgren (1906-1998), Matthew Black, (1908-1994), Barbara Aland (1937-present), and Carlo Maria Martini (1927-2012).

[117] Tregelles, *An Account of the Printed Text of the Greek New Testament*, 174.

[118] Westcott and Hort, *Introduction to the New Testament in the Original Greek*, 1.

[119] Metzger, *The Text of the New Testament*, v.

[120] J. K. Elliott, *New Testament Textual Criticism: The Application of Thoroughgoing Principles: Essays on Manuscripts and Textual Variation*, 592.

to be the consensus at one of the sessions of the 1998 SBL conference in Orlando, where the question of whether the original text was an achievable goal received generally negative responses."[121]

We strongly disagree. The goal of textual criticism had been and still should be **to restore** the New Testament Greek text **in every word that was originally penned** by the New Testament authors, in a critical edition. If we are aiming only "to plot the changes in the history of the text," as Elliott put it, we are unable to do so precisely at the time when we have the greatest need to see what happened, i.e. soon after the NT books were first published, if we actually deny and rob ourselves of any chance to recover the original. Then we must admit either that we can never have the complete word of God (the new position), or that any and potentially every quality Greek witness must be considered the word of God. The latter might even be said of a quality version, or at least of readings clearly inferred from such a version. In reality, however, any manuscript that departs from the original in its witness is more or less damaged goods.

We obviously do not think such pessimism is the necessary or inevitable response. In looking at the numbers above as to the certainty level of the restoration of the original Greek New Testament, we have come a long way since John Fell (1625-1686). A spot comparison of changes in ratings between GNT5 and previous GNT editions indicates that the level of certainty is increasing in most cases, and when it does not, the preference tends toward the earliest and most reliable manuscripts.[122] To set aside the primary goal of textual criticism now would be an insult to the lives of many textual scholars who preceded us, not to mention to the authors who penned the New Testament books and the Almighty God who inspired them.

---

[121] Ibid. 592.

[122] Sample comparisons of the General Epistles in GNT5 with previous GNT editions led to this conclusion. When the level of certainty decreased—which was infrequent compared to the reverse—the trend seemed to be that more weight was being given to 03 and/or 01 in opposition to internal factors. It is also expected that certainty levels will increase with the use of the CBGM (discussed in detail below).

Related Books by Andrews

Bibliography

Aland, Kurt and Barbara. 1987. *The Text of the New Testament.* Grand Rapids: Eerdmans.

Andrews, Edward D, and Don Wilkins. 2017. *THE TEXT OF THE NEW TESTAMENT: The Science and Art of Textual Criticism.* Cambridge: Christian Publishing House.

Archer, Gleason L. 1982. *New International Encyclopedia of Bible Difficulties, Zondervan's Understand the Bible Reference Series.* Zondervan Publishing House: Grand Rapids, MI.

Arndt, William, Frederick W. Danker, and Walter Bauer. 2000. *A Greek-English Lexicon of the New Testament and Other Early Christian Literature. 3rd ed.* . Chicago: University of Chicago Press.

Bercot, David W. 1998. *A Dictionary of Early Christian Beliefs.* Peabody: Hendrickson.

Burgon, John W., and Edward Miller. 1896. *The Causes of the Corruption of the Traditional Text of the Holy Gospels.* London: George Bell and Sons.

Colwell, Ernest C. 1969. *Method in Evaluating Scribal Habits: A Study of P45, P66, P75, in Studies in Methodology in Textual Criticism of the New Testament, New Testament Tools and Studies 9.* Leiden: Brill.

Comfort, Philip W. 2005. *Encountering the Manuscripts: An Introduction to New Testament Paleography & Textual Criticism.* Grand Rapids, MI: B&H Academic.

—. 2008. *New Testament Text and Translation Commentary.* Carol Stream: Tyndale House Publishers.

—. 1992. *The Quest for the Original Text of the New Testament.* Eugene, Oregon: Wipf and Stock Publishers.

Comfort, Philip, and David Barret. 2001. *The Text of the Earliest New Testament Greek Manuscripts.* Wheaton: Tyndale House Publishers.

Elwell, Walter A, and Philip Wesley Comfort. 2001. *Tyndale Bible Dictionary.* Wheaton: Tyndale House Publishers.

Elwell, Walter A. 2001. *Evangelical Dictionary of Theology (Second Edition).* Grand Rapids: Baker Academic.

Gamble, Harry Y. 1997. *Books and Readers in the Early Church: A History of Early Christian Texts.* New Haven and London: Yale University Press.

Greenlee, J Harold. 1995. *Introduction to New Testament Textual Criticism.* Peabody: Hendrickson.

Holmes, Michael William. 2006. *"The Apostolic Fathers: Greek Texts and English Translations".* Grand Rapids, MI: Baker Books.

Kenyon Sr., Frederic G. 1896. *Our Bible and the Ancient Manuscripts: Being a History of the Text and Its Translations.* London: Eyre & Spottiswood.

Liddell, Henry George et al.,. 1996. *A Greek-English Lexicon .* Oxford: Clarendon Press.

Metzger, Bruce M. 1994. *A Textual Commentary on the Greek New Testament.* New York: United Bible Society.

Metzger, Bruce M., and Bart D. Ehrman. 1964, 1968, 1992, 2005. *The Text of the New Testament: Its Transmission, Corruption, and Transmission.* New York: Oxford University Press.

Mounce, William D. 2006. *Mounce's Complete Expository Dictionary of Old & New Testament Words.* Grand Rapids, MI: Zondervan.

Pagels, Elaine. 1989. *The Gnostic Gospels.* New York: Vintage.

Pickering, Wilbur. 1980. *The Identity of the New Testament Text (rev. ed.).* Nashville: Nelson.

Robertson, A. T. 1925. *An Introduction to the Textual Criticism of the New Testament.* London: Hodder & Stoughton.

Royse, James Ronald. 1981. *Scribal Habits in Early Greek New Testament Papyri (Ph.D. diss.,).* Berkeley, CA: Graduate Theological Union.

Swanson, James. 1997. *Dictionary of Biblical Languages with Semantic Domains: Greek (New Testament).* Oak Harbor: Logos Research Systems.

Vine, W. E., Merrill F. Unger, and William White Jr. 1996. *Vine's Complete Expository Dictionary of Old and New Testament Words.* Nashville, TN: T. Nelson.

Wegner, Paul D. 2006. *A Student's Guide to Textual Criticism of the Bible: Its History Methods & Results.* Downers Grove: InterVarsity Press.

Wood, D R W. 1996. *New Bible Dictionary (Third Edition).* Downers Grove: InterVarsity Press.

Zodhiates, Spiros. 2000, c1992, c1993. *The Complete Word Study Dictionary: New Testament.* Chattanooga: AMG Publishers.

46508192R00081

Printed in Poland
by Amazon Fulfillment
Poland Sp. z o.o., Wrocław